Due Process of Law

Due Process of Law

A Brief History

John V. Orth

University Press of Kansas

Published by the University Press of Kansas (Lawrence, Kansas 66049),
which was organized by the Kansas Board of Regents and is operated
and funded by Emporia State University, Fort Hays State University,
Kansas State University, Pittsburg State University, the University of Kansas,
and Wichita State University

Library of Congress Cataloging-in-Publication Data

Orth, John V.

Due process of law : a brief history / John V. Orth.

p. cm.

Includes bibliographical references and index.

ISBN 0-7006-1241-6 (cloth : alk. paper) —

ISBN 0-7006-1242-4 (pbk. : alk. paper)

1. Due process of law — United States. I. Title.

KF4765 .O78 2003   347.73'05—dc21   2002015334

British Library Cataloguing in Publication Data is available.

Printed in the United States of America

10 9 8 7 6 5 4 3 2

The paper used in this publication meets the minimum requirements
of the American National Standard for Permanence of Paper for Printed
Library Materials z39.48-1984.

Contents

Preface

What you are about to read concerning the law and history of due process is as accurate as I can make it, but it is not the way the story is usually told. For one thing, although I have endeavored to read as many due process cases as possible, I have made no attempt to describe all or even most of them in this book. Other scholars have already done that, and their works are listed in the bibliography. Nor have I been concerned with judicial personalities; this is not a study in the intellectual biographies of the judges who made the law of due process. A few of the cases were decided over vigorous dissents, including some made famous by later scholarship. Although this suggests that individual cases could have come out the other way, it does not indicate, at least to me, that the broad outlines of the story would have been altered with one judge more or less.

The roots of due process run too deep in the law and legal profession. So, the details of who dissented and why are not included in the text but, when relevant, are put in the footnotes for those who are interested.

Furthermore, I have approached the subject in an unconventional way by looking at the hypothetical cases that served as paradigms in the legal history of due process. Judges were deciding cases long before there were written constitutions, or even very many statutes; and cases, to be decided, must be reduced to simple, almost abstract form, then compared and contrasted with other cases whose results are already known. Exemplary cases provided easy-to-remember compendia of the law, handy reference points in the resolution of difficult disputes. Although the fact is sometimes overlooked, constitutional law developed in much the same way, despite the presence of an authoritative text.

Legal rules can seem innumerable, and legal theory, particularly law school theory, can become supersophisticated, but lawyers and judges often have to operate in a rough-and-ready way. As the Harvard Law School dean C. C. Langdell observed more than a century ago, "The number of fundamental legal doctrines is much less than is commonly supposed; the many different guises in which the same doctrine is constantly making its appearance, and the great extent to which legal treatises are a repetition of each other, being the cause of much misapprehension." Illustrative cases, few in number but useful reminders of fundamental principles, long formed part of every lawyer's stock-in-trade; to some extent, they still do. The history of due process can be understood as the progression and development of these paradigm cases.

There are many reasons for studying legal history, among them the desire to find precedents for future decisions. Legal scholars often look to the past as part of a project to propose a particular direction for future development. Though this book may prove helpful in the search for precedents, it was not written for that purpose. To make the text more readable, case names are kept to a minimum, and no attempt is made to capture every nuance of doctrine. Cases refining, clarifying, or qualifying leading cases are not necessarily included, as befits a "short history."

Nor was this project undertaken, as some legal scholarship occasionally is, particularly in the due process area, in order to decry the judicial mistakes of the past and tell a cautionary tale for the present. This book was written with the full understanding that many of the old cases were controversial when decided and that many of the recent cases still are; judgments of right and wrong, legal as well as moral, can—indeed, should—be made, but that was not my purpose here. Instead, my goal was simply to explain how the seemingly uncomplicated phrase "due process of law" came to have such complicated (and contested) meanings. As I said in an earlier book, concerned with a different part of the Constitution, if we can understand how we got here, we will understand more comprehensively where we are.

"Due process of law" has long been part of our constitutional vocabulary; few phrases are more important. But the words themselves, while suggestive, are hardly self-explanatory. Judges and lawyers have struggled, literally for hundreds of years, to give them content in specific cases. Their results have not always been universally accepted, and consensus, when achieved, has rarely endured for long. The attempt to realize the ideal in ever-changing conditions is probably an inescapable part of our legal tradition, and one from which we should hesitate to escape by a peremptory announcement that the demands of due process have been ascertained once and for all.

A common starting place for much American constitutional history is a resort to the "intent of the Founders," as if the drafters of our basic constitutional texts had thought of everything. Subsequent judicial decisions are then tested for fidelity to this supposed "original intent." A sympathetic commentator can usually find consistency; a critic will find perversions. The starting point for this book, by contrast, is the common law method of decision making. This approach was chosen for the simple reason that the demands of due process are much older than any constitutional text. The American Founders adopted the phrase and concept from preexisting English common law. Not only was due process a common law concept to begin with, it remained subject to common law development by judges trained in the common law way of doing things. The approach here adopted is accordingly to focus less on texts and imputed intention and more on the simple exemplary cases used to illustrate the great common law formula, "due process of law."

A Note to Readers

This book is written to be read "above the line," that is, above the line separating footnotes and text. Nothing essential to the story is in the footnotes, and the ordinary reader may safely disregard them. What the notes contain are citations for cases mentioned in the text, references to sources for readers who wish to learn more about a particular point, and occasional digressions or clarifications to explain myself more fully to those with professional training in law or history.

Introduction.
Getting Down to Cases

> Where there are no fixed established maxims of law, the
> citizens are in the same situation as farmers, whose lands are not
> divided by any monuments or known bounds. They will be very
> likely to go to law, and very unlikely to obtain satisfactory
> decisions. Maxims of law are like landmarks.
>
> JEREMIAH SMITH (1805)

The judges made the common law in their decisions of individual cases. Not only did a decision in one case resolve a specific dispute, but it also provided a rule to guide the decision of other, similar cases.[1] "Like cases should be decided

[1]In legal jargon the dispute-resolution effect of a judicial decision is labeled *res judicata:* once finally resolved, an individual dispute becomes a "thing adjudged" and may not be relitigated. The rule-making effect is called *stare decisis:* the judges should "stand by the decision" in prior cases and apply the same rule in the future. See John V. Orth, "The Secret Sources of Judicial Power" (unpublished).

alike" is perhaps the fundamental rule of justice.[2] Children instinctively recognize its force and implicitly appeal to it when they say, "You let *him* do it!" Generalizing the rule from the case is the common law lawyer's first skill, and the second is closely related to it: distinguishing like from unlike cases. Parents rely on the latter when they respond, "It's not the same thing!" or "You're not like him!"

The paradox at the heart of the history of the common law is that the decision seems to come before the rule; cases are decided before the law is made. The truth, which the early judges implicitly recognized, is that a generalized sense of justice precedes the case; the need to decide the specific dispute only forces a specific formulation of the rule. The problem is not confined to the remote past; even today, judges occasionally confront novel disputes for which no clear precedent or statute is available as a guide to decision, what they call "cases of first instance." One wise twentieth-century judge explained the process in such cases: "The system of lawmaking by judicial decisions which supply the rule for transactions closed before the decision was announced would indeed be intolerable in its hardship and oppression if natural law, in the sense in which I have used the term, did not supply the main rule of judgment to the judge when precedent and custom

---

[2]Sir Edward Coke described as "one of the Maximes of the Common Law" that "wheresoever there is the like reason, there is the like law" (see *Commentary upon Littleton* [1628], London, 1911a).

fail or are displaced."[3] Natural law, in one sense or another, has guided common law judges since the Middle Ages.

Keeping in mind the imperative need to decide the cases presented to them, and the absence in many early cases of any clearly formulated rules to guide them, one can easily appreciate the value to the judges of simple legal maxims, brief rules of thumb encapsulating years of experience. Just as proverbs have been called the philosophy of the common people, so legal maxims once figured prominently in the judges' decisions of leading cases. Indeed, the founding reports of the common law display a greater reliance on maxims than on precedents.

Legal literature before the modern era was remarkably limited; other than unofficial reports of cases prepared by lawyers for sale to other lawyers, little was available, even as late as the time of William Shakespeare. Sir Francis Bacon, Shakespeare's great contemporary, who planned an ambitious restatement of the common law to make it presentable by Renaissance standards, began by collecting legal maxims. From the hundreds he found, Bacon selected

---

[3]Benjamin N. Cardozo, *The Nature of the Judicial Process* (New Haven: Yale University Press, 1921), 142. Cardozo used "natural law" in a loose sense to describe the social understandings common to society. The resort to natural law does not permit the judge to exercise an unconstrained discretion but "a discretion informed by tradition, methodized by analogy, disciplined by system, and subordinated to 'the primordial necessity of order in the social life'" (141).

twenty-five for publication, carefully done up in Latin, the learned language of the day. Bacon's *Maxims of the Law* (1630) quickly became a classic, consulted and cited in court for centuries.[4] Although legal literature became more sophisticated over the years, legal maxims maintained their popularity. In the nineteenth century an extensive collection by the English lawyer and academic Herbert Broom, which he candidly admitted had been drawn from the many previous collections, including Bacon's, was widely used; as late as 1924 an updated American edition of *Broom's Maxims* was produced.[5]

Thinking in maxims characterized the common law into the modern era, until the appearance of legal treatises in the nineteenth century and the triumph of modern legal education in the twentieth century made their use unfashionable. University law professors and university-trained lawyers increasingly found maxims simplistic, inadequate to express their sophisticated legal doctrines. But academic scorn did not cause maxims to disappear altogether from practice or judicial opinions; increasingly, however, they

---

[4]Francis Bacon, *A Collection of Some Principall Rules and Maximes of the Common Law,* in *The Elements of the Common Lawes of England* (London, 1630). For ninety-seven "aphorisms" of Bacon's own devising, see *Examples of a Treatise on Universal Justice.* See also Catherine Drinker Bowen, *Francis Bacon, The Temper of the Man* (Boston: Little, Brown, 1963), 86–87.

[5]See William S. Holdsworth, *A History of English Law* (London: Methuen, 1938), 12: 188–91 and 15: 368.

were used not so much to state the legal rule at the beginning as to summarize the conclusion at the end. Justice Oliver Wendell Holmes's notable facility at capping his decisions with stunning epigrams was not only an inheritance from his literary father; it was also a mark of the consummate common law judge.

Maxims encapsulate rules and serve as handy illustrations of legal principles; they may be called, borrowing a term now fashionable in some academic discourse, "paradigms."[6] Just as paradigms inform scientific epochs and "paradigm shifts" mark revolutions in science, so legal maxims, their progression and development, can describe and facilitate legal change. One of the most frequently asked questions in American constitutional history has been, what is required by the constitutional guarantee of "due process of law"? The phrase appears twice in the U.S. Constitution—in the Fifth Amendment in the Bill of Rights, which prohibits the federal government from depriving any person of "life, liberty,

[6]See Thomas S. Kuhn, *The Structure of Scientific Revolutions,* 2d ed. (Chicago: University of Chicago Press, 1970), 175. Kuhn admits to using "paradigm" in two different senses: "On the one hand, it stands for the entire constellation of beliefs, values, techniques, and so on shared by the members of a given community. On the other, it denotes one sort of element in that constellation, the concrete puzzle-solutions which, employed as models or examples, can replace explicit rules as a basis for the solution of the remaining puzzles of normal science." See also John V. Orth, "Taking from A and Giving to B: Substantive Due Process and the Case of the Shifting Paradigm," *Constitutional Commentary* 14 (1997): 337–45.

or property, without due process of law,"[7] and in the Four-teenth Amendment, adopted almost one hundred years later in the aftermath of the Civil War, which extends the same prohibition to the states: "No State shall . . . deprive any person of life, liberty, or property, without due process of law." What exactly does due process require? General words remain only abstractions until applied in specific cases; maxims or paradigmatic cases can help bridge the gap between general and specific.

Can a law make a man a judge in his own case? Can a law take the property of A and give it to B? These questions more than any others were used over the centuries to illuminate the demands of due process. They are not questions asked only in American law; they can arise in any legal system. And "due process of law" was not a phrase invented by American constitution-writers: it was picked up by them from the rich tradition of English constitutionalism in which they were formed. From this perspective, the War of American Independence can be regarded as a civil war within the British Empire over the meaning and future course of the British constitution. Unlike their French counterparts a few years later, American Revolutionaries did not lay claim to "the rights of man" but to "the rights of Englishmen."

---

[7] The words of the Fifth Amendment alone do not limit its effect, but an early Supreme Court case held that it, as well as all the other amendments in the Bill of Rights, apply only to the federal government. See *Barron v. Baltimore*, 32 U.S. (7 Pet.) 243 (1833).

English rights were first memorably expressed in Magna Carta in 1215. Among many other things, the notorious King John was forced by his rebellious barons to promise that "nullus liber homo capiatur, vel imprisonetur, aut disseisiatur, aut utlagetur, aut exulatur, aut aliquo modo destruatur, nec super eum ibimus, nec super eum mittemus, nisi per legale judicium parium suorum vel per legem terrae" (no free man shall be taken or imprisoned or disseised or outlawed or exiled, or in any way ruined, nor will we go or send against him, except by the lawful judgment of his peers or by the law of the land).[8] What exactly that meant in the Middle Ages is not completely clear, and scholars continue to debate the point. Over the ensuing centuries, Magna Carta was even lost sight of temporarily, but in the constitutional controversies of the seventeenth century, as other English monarchs encroached on English liberties, it was rediscovered and gained renewed prominence.

Sir Edward Coke, a contemporary of Bacon and Shakespeare, wrote influential commentaries on English statutes, restating and in the process enlarging the demands of Magna Carta: the "law of the land," Coke said, meant the

[8]Magna Carta, § 39. I have, with one exception, used the Latin text and translation in J. C. Holt, *Magna Carta* (Cambridge: Cambridge University Press, 1965), 326–27. For "legum terre" I have substituted "legem terrae" because years of subsequent usage gave the original Medieval Latin a more classical look.

common law, and the common law required "due process."[9] The earliest American state constitutions clung to the words of the Great Charter and safeguarded the "law of the land"; a few of them still do.[10] But the drafters of the federal Bill of Rights opted for Coke's phrase, and "due process of law" has been standard American usage ever since. Most state constitutions today follow the federal example,[11] and those that continue to guarantee the "law of the land" are routinely interpreted to require the same thing.[12]

In its English origin the guarantee of due process (or the law of the land) was a restraint on the sovereign: before King John or his royal officers could take action against a person, certain procedures had to be followed, procedures designed to ensure fairness. Fair procedures are still at the

[9]Edward Coke, *Institutes of the Laws of England* (London, 1648), 2: 50. Coke derived the phrase from a statute in "Law French," the vernacular of English law for three centuries following the Norman Conquest, citing 25 Edw. 3, st. 5, c. 4 (1350): "en due manere ou process fait sur brief original a la commune lei." See William S. Holdsworth, *A History of English Law,* 7th ed. (London: Methuen, 1956), 1: 59–63.

[10]E.g., Maryland Constitution, Declaration of Rights, Art. 24 (original in Md. Const. of 1776, Decl. of Rts., § 21); North Carolina Constitution, Art. 1, § 19 (original in N.C. Const. of 1776, Decl. of Rts., § 4). See John V. Orth, *The North Carolina State Constitution: A Reference Guide* (Westport, Conn.: Greenwood Press, 1993), 41–44.

[11]E.g., California Constitution, Art. 1, § 7.

[12]E.g., *Parish v. East Coast Cedar Co.,* 45 S.E. 768, 770 (N.C. 1903) ("it is well settled that the phrases 'due process of law' and 'the law of the land' mean identically the same thing, and the authorities on each are cited interchangeably"), and *Eason v. Spence,* 61 S.E.2d 617 (N.C. 1950) (same).

heart of due process today;[13] in modern parlance they are often expressed by the somewhat different phrase, "the rule of law."[14] Although a number of elements constitute the rule of law, the procedural essentials can be encapsulated in the requirement of an accessible, impartial, and effective decision maker or, to put it simply, a good judge. Can a law make a man a judge in his own case? The question can be used to test the procedural fairness of any legal system by highlighting one of its most essential features, whether cases are decided by an independent decision maker, one with no personal stake in the outcome and no fear of retribution from the powers that be if the case is decided one way or the other. It can be used to test, in other words, whether the system guarantees the rule of law; in the common law system it signifies respect for the traditional procedures of the "law of the land" or "due process of law."

Six hundred and fifty years after Magna Carta, in the last quarter of the nineteenth century, due process in America had come to include significant constitutional limitations on legislative power as well. No longer exclusively concerned with how the executive proceeded, due process had developed a concern with what the legislature did; that is, due process had acquired a substantive dimension. The U.S.

[13]John E. Nowak et al., *Constitutional Law*, 2d ed. (St. Paul, Minn.: West Publishing Company, 1983), 557: "The essential guarantee of the due process clause is that of fairness."

[14]See John V. Orth, "Exporting the Rule of Law," *North Carolina Journal of International Law* 24 (1998): 71–82.

Supreme Court justice Samuel Miller had the historical perspective to recognize the contrast. In 1878 in *Davidson v. New Orleans* he wrote on behalf of the Court: "It is easy to see that when the great barons of England wrung from King John, at the point of the sword, the concession that neither their lives nor their property should be disposed of by the crown, except as provided by the law of the land, they meant by 'law of the land' the ancient and customary laws of the English people, or laws enacted by the Parliament of which those barons were a controlling element. It was not in their minds, therefore, to protect themselves against the enactment of laws by the Parliament of England."[15] But, he continued, the Fourteenth Amendment directed the Supreme Court's attention to action by the states. "Can a State make anything due process of law which, by its own legislation, it chooses to declare such?"[16] he asked rhetorically, and promptly answered on behalf of his brethren: "To affirm this is to hold that the prohibition to the States is of no avail, or has no application where the invasion of private rights is effected under the forms of State legislation. It

[15]96 U.S. 102 (1878). Modern scholars have determined that it is anachronistic to speak of "parliament" as a legislature at the time of Magna Carta (1215). "The word has been traced back to Henry II's reign [1154–1189], but it was first used by the chronicler Matthew Paris to describe such a meeting [of the great council] in 1239." See Bryce Lyon, *A Constitutional and Legal History of Medieval England* (New York: Harper and Brothers, 1960), 413.

[16]96 U.S. 97, 102.

seems to us that a statute which declares in terms, and without more, that the full and exclusive title of a described piece of land, which is now in A, shall be and is hereby vested in B, would, if effectual, deprive A of his property without due process of law, within the meaning of the constitutional provision."[17] Taking from A and giving to B had become, in other words, the shorthand to describe what substantive due process was designed to prevent. As one modern scholar put it, quoting *Davidson,* the A-to-B paradigm was "every nineteenth century lawyer's favorite example of an unconstitutional statute—albeit one that was unconstitutional for various different reasons."[18]

Making a man a judge in his own case was a bad thing, all could agree. So was taking from A and giving to B, but what the problem was exactly was not so clear. A great many cases, some of them quite different, could be comprehended within the seemingly simple A-to-B paradigm, and that ambiguity allowed a good deal of out-of-sight judicial development. At first, the taking was assumed to involve A's property: the classic formula was, in fact, as Justice Miller put it, a law that took A's *land* and gave it to B. Law has always been about power, and in medieval England, at the

---

[17]Ibid. Because the court upheld the challenged legislation in *Davidson,* the A-to-B discussion was not strictly necessary to the decision of the case but was only dictum. Dictum became holding in *Missouri Pacific Railway Co. v. Nebraska,* 164 U.S. 403, 417 (1896).

[18]John Harrison, "Substantive Due Process and the Constitutional Text," *Virginia Law Review* 83 (1997): 493, 506.

origin of the common law, power was intimately tied up with land ownership, so the early common law showed a precocious interest in property. For centuries, land law remained at the center of things, elaborated into an increasingly complex system with its own vocabulary and concepts, some of them quite fantastic.[19] But property was never confined to land, and as concepts of property expanded over time to include a host of intangible interests, so did the scope of due process.

Beginning in the eighteenth century, in the years before the American Revolution, the common law was forced to confront new economic arrangements with momentous consequences for the distribution of power within society. International trade, spurred by Britain's world-girdling empire, required the organization of production and the transportation of goods over vast distances. Frontier conditions in America put unheard of amounts of land on the market, much of it purchased on installment contracts or with complicated loan agreements. In the mobilization of the new productive forces, contract assumed an importance that was to rival, if not surpass, property; wealth and power now lay in agreements as much as in ownership. As the emphasis of the common law shifted from property to contract, so the

---

[19]See, e.g., John V. Orth, "After the Revolution: 'Reform' of the Law of Inheritance," *Law and History Review* 10 (1992): 33–44; "Requiem for the Rule in Shelley's Case," *North Carolina Law Review* 67 (1988): 681–93; "Does the Fee Tail Exist in North Carolina?" *Wake Forest Law Review* 23 (1988): 767–95.

cases involving due process shifted as well. If the law was to protect contract as zealously as it protected property, a new view of due process was required. Liberty, it was recalled, was covered as well as property, and concern about taking away A's property was soon rivaled by concern about taking away A's liberty, specifically A's liberty to enter into enforceable agreements or, as it was more commonly called, A's freedom of contract.[20]

The shift from property to contract by no means marked the end of the story. In time, as experience with takings accumulated, it appeared that what was taken and who got it were less important than that any kind of taking had occurred. The new focus on individual agreement had redirected attention away from things and toward persons. Liberated from a preoccupation with property, the law increasingly recognized less tangible interests, at first in labor but later in private matters such as reproductive rights. In the twentieth century, as the emphasis in the law shifted from contract to civil rights, so the cases shifted from concern with interfering with A's freedom of contract to concern with interfering with A's freedom in other regards.

Beginning as the history of proper procedure, the history of due process became the history of substantive guarantees as well. Procedure is a perennial concern of the courts, but

[20]See John V. Orth, "Contract and the Common Law," in *The State and Freedom of Contract,* ed. Harry N. Scheiber (Stanford: Stanford University Press, 1998), 44–65.

substance varies with the times, as economic and social demands come and go. Maxims and simple exemplary cases (paradigms) once registered this progression. In the chapters that follow we shall look more closely at the cases of "making a man a judge in his own case" and "taking from A and giving to B" and shall explore the hidden ambiguity in the taking paradigm that permitted a great deal of change while maintaining the appearance of continuity. Finally, we shall observe how substantive due process changed its focus from economic rights, whether property or contract, and concentrated instead on noneconomic or social rights.

Case I. Making a Man a Judge in His Own Case: Procedural Due Process

And what my Lord Coke says in *Dr. Bonham's Case* in his 8 Co. is far from any extravagancy, for it is a very reasonable and true saying, that if an Act of Parliament should ordain that the same person should be party and Judge, or, which is the same thing, Judge in his own cause, it would be a void Act of Parliament; for it is impossible that one should be Judge and party, for the Judge is to determine between party and party, or between the Government and the party; and an Act of Parliament can do no wrong, though it may do several things that look pretty odd; for it may discharge one from his allegiance of the Government he lives under, and restore him to the state of nature; but it cannot make one who lives under a Government Judge and party.

SIR JOHN HOLT, C.J. (1701)

Can a law make a man a judge in his own case? The question seems almost to answer itself. Judging requires a degree of impartiality, and a judge with a stake in the outcome of a case would necessarily be too involved to be impartial. "Il n'est pas permis au plus équitable homme du monde d'être juge en sa cause" (the fairest man in the world is not allowed to be a judge in his own cause), Blaise Pascal observed in his famous *Pensées* (1670).[1] And James Madison in the justly celebrated *Federalist* no. 10 declared that "no man is allowed to be a judge in his own cause, because his interest would certainly bias his judgment, and, not improbably, corrupt his integrity."[2] At first, it is difficult to take the question seriously if asked about a society committed to the rule of law, one alert to what are now called "conflicts of interest." Only in a dictatorship, and a pretty bad one at that, would the situation seem to arise at all. Yet the matter is more complicated than it first appears, and the question has been asked repeatedly in the history of the common law, not always getting the expected answer. It has even been used to define the great constitutional moments in English and American history.

The problem of a man claiming jurisdiction in his own case appears in the very first book on English law ever printed, a book so old that it was written in "Law French," the vernacular of English courts for three centuries follow-

---

[1]Blaise Pascal, *Pensées* (1670), frag. 44. "Cause" in French and English is simply the technical word for a legal proceeding or "case."

[2]Alexander Hamilton, James Madison, and John Jay, *The Federalist Papers*, ed. Benjamin Wright (Cambridge: Harvard University Press, 1961), 131. See Gordon S. Wood, "The Origins of American Democracy, or How the People Became Judges in their Own Causes," *Cleveland State Law Review* 47 (1999): 309–22.

ing the Norman Conquest in 1066. Prompted perhaps by an actual case, Sir Thomas Littleton, in his *Tenures,* a short treatise on English land law of about 1481, poses the question: suppose a man alleged that it was the custom of his manor that he as lord could distrain (that is, seize) cattle that strayed onto his land and keep them until their owner paid him a fine in the amount he assessed for the damage they had caused. One can easily see how in early days, when national institutions were weak and the manor was a self-contained unit, such a custom could arise. If the lord were fair-minded, particularly if he took counsel with his tenants, the fine might well be just, but as royal justice spread over England and as more sophisticated, or worldly wise, minds considered the question, the potential for abuse appeared most prominent. As Littleton put it, "If he had dammages but to the value of a halfpeny, he might assess and have therefore an hundred pound, which should be against reason."[3] Reason, in Littleton's view, is the test of custom, a custom claiming the force of law.[4] Measured by reason, this custom fails, "pur ceo que il est encounter reason, que si tort soit fait a un home, que il de ceo serroit son judge demesne"

---

[3] Thomas Littleton, *Tenures,* § 212, "s'il avoit dammages forsque al value d'un mail, il puissoit assesser et aver pur ceo C. lib." (translation in text by Sir Edward Coke).

[4] Custom was still a source of law hundreds of years later, and reasonableness one of its requisites. See William Blackstone, *Commentaries on the Laws of England* (Oxford, 1765), 1: 77 (citing Littleton's *Tenures,* § 212). Indeed, it remains a source of law today. See *State ex rel. Thornton v. Hay,* 462 P.2d 671 (Or. 1969) (citing Blackstone).

(because it is against reason, that if wrong be done any man, that he thereof should be his own judge).[5]

More than a century later, the question of making a man a judge in his own case was posed in a new and more troublesome form. In 1610 Dr. Thomas Bonham was charged by the Royal College of Physicians with practicing physic in London without a license.[6] As permitted by its royal charter, which had been repeatedly confirmed by acts of Parliament, the college tried Bonham in its own court. Finding him guilty, it imposed a sentence of fine and imprisonment, and as permitted by its charter it proposed to pocket half the fine. An appeal in the modern sense was not permitted at that time, so Bonham challenged his confinement by an action for false imprisonment. Sir Edward Coke, then chief justice of the Court of Common Pleas, prepared an elaborate summary of the court's decision as part of his series of influential law reports.[7] Carefully read-

[5]Littleton, *Tenures,* § 212. For a discussion of the maxim's use before Littleton, see D. E. C. Yale, "*Iudex in Propria Causa:* An Historical Excursus," *Cambridge Law Journal* 33 (1974): 80–96.

[6]The literature on *Dr. Bonham's Case* is voluminous. For the most detailed account of the facts, see Harold J. Cook, "Against Common Right and Reason: The Royal College of Physicians Versus Doctor Thomas Bonham," *American Journal of Legal History* 29 (1985): 301–22. For a thorough analysis of Coke's opinion in the case, see James R. Stoner Jr., *Common Law and Liberal Theory: Coke, Hobbes, and the Origins of American Constitutionalism* (Lawrence: University Press of Kansas, 1992), 48–62.

[7]Coke's Reports, cited as Co. Rep. or Co., were for a long time referred to simply as "the Reports." See *Black's Law Dictionary,* 4th ed., rev. (St. Paul, Minn.: West Publishing Company, 1968), 1465.

ing the charter, the court found that the college was not in fact empowered to imprison for unlicensed practice but only for malpractice, which had not been alleged, and ruled in Bonham's favor.

Although technically the question of Bonham's fine was not before the court, Coke addressed it anyway, acidly commenting that the physicians "cannot be judges, ministers, and parties; judges to give sentence or judgment; ministers to make summons; and parties to have the moiety [half] of the forfeiture." He capped his comment in classic fashion with a Latin maxim, drawn partly from Roman law: "aliquis non debet esse judex in propria causa, imo iniquum est aliquem suae rei esse judicem" (because someone ought not be a judge in his own cause, for it is unfair for someone to be a judge in his own affairs).[8] Coke may well have been thinking of Littleton when he wrote those words; he certainly admired Littleton's book, praising it extravagantly as "the ornament of the common law," "the most perfect and absolute work ever written in any humane science," "a work of as absolute perfection in its kind, and as free from error, as any book that I have known to be written of any humane

[8]*Dr. Bonham's Case,* 8 Co. Rep. 107a, 118a, 77 Eng. Rep. 638, 652 (1610). For the Roman law original, see *Digest* 5.1.17: "Iulianus ait, si alter ex litigatoribus iudicem solum heredem uel ex parte fecerit, alius iudex necessario sumendus est, quia iniquum est aliquem suae rei iudicem fieri." (Julian says that if one of the litigants has made the judge heir to all or part of his estate, another judge must of necessity be appointed, because it is unfair to make someone judge in his own affairs).

learning."[9] Years later Coke published a definitive commentary on Littleton's *Tenures,* which became a legal classic in its own right, known to generations of lawyers as "Coke on Littleton," cited simply "Co. Litt.," but he was probably already at work on his elaborate notes at the time of *Dr. Bonham's Case.* To Littleton's text Coke appended the very phrase he had used in discharging *Bonham:* "For it is a maxime in law, *aliquis non debet esse judex in propria causa*" (someone ought not be a judge in his own cause).[10]

Generalizing from the specifics in *Dr. Bonham's Case,* Coke added a few words that have echoed down the centuries, resounding more loudly in fact in America than in England: "And it appears in our books, that in many cases, the common law will controul Acts of Parliament, and sometimes adjudge them to be utterly void: for when an Act of Parliament is against common right and reason, or repugnant, or impossible to be performed, the common law will controul it, and adjudge such Act to be void."[11] In colonial America the idea was succinctly restated: "An act contrary to the constitution is void."[12] When those words were first uttered, the English

---

[9]Edward Coke, *Commentary upon Littleton* (1628), preface, xxxvii. Coke's *Commentary upon Littleton* is also known as the first volume of his *Institutes of the Laws of England.*

[10]Ibid., 141a. Coke also cited some of the same English authorities he had used in *Dr. Bonham's Case.*

[11]8 Co. Rep. 107a, 118a, 77 Eng. Rep. 638, 652.

[12]James Otis Jr., counsel for defendants, in *Paxton's Case* (1761)— better known as the *Writs of Assistance Case,* a cause célèbre before the

constitution was, as it still is, an ill-defined collection of traditional practices and important statutes.[13] Later, after American Independence, U.S. chief justice John Marshall used almost the same words, "a law repugnant to the constitution is void," but with a much more specific reference; this time the constitution in question was a single document, the new Constitution of the United States.[14] This was indeed the founding statement of judicial review, the power of an American court to declare whether a legislative act is constitutional, whether what appears to be a law is a law in fact.

Illustrating the "many cases" in which Coke claimed the common law had invalidated parliamentary statutes, he returned obsessively to the judge in his own case: "So, if any Act of Parliament gives to any to hold, or to have conusans [cognizance] of all manner of pleas arising before him

---

American Revolution—quoted in M. H. Smith, *The Writs of Assistance Case* (Berkeley: University of California Press, 1978), 364, 555 (all capital letters in original).

[13]Membership in the European Union is adding content to the English Constitution, and today the European Court of Human Rights might have something to say about violations of the rule of law, including making a man a judge in his own case. See, generally, Nuala Mole, "International Law, the Individual, and A. W. Brian Simpson's Contribution to the Defence of Human Rights," in *Human Rights and Legal History: Essays in Honour of Brian Simpson*, ed. Katherine O'Donovan and Gerry Rubin (Oxford: Oxford University Press, 2000), 13–28.

[14]*Marbury v. Madison,* 5 U.S. (1 Cranch) 137, 180 (1803). Marshall himself may have retained a more expansive understanding of the word "constitution," but in *Marbury* he was construing a specific provision of the U.S.

within his manor of D., yet he shall hold no plea, to which he himself is a party," citing once again the Latin maxim: "iniquum est aliquem suae rei esse judicem" (it is unfair for someone to be a judge in his own affairs).[15]

When faulting the Royal College of Physicians' disciplinary procedure, Coke was naturally reminded of Littleton's comment from more than a century earlier. In both the case of the cattle straying onto the lord's land and the case of the doctor infringing a medical monopoly, the party who collects the fine is also the party who suffered the wrong. As Littleton said, "It is against reason, that if wrong be done any man, that he thereof should be his own judge." To that extent the cases are certainly alike and should be decided alike. But the cases are also different. Littleton was describing a case in which the common law was testing a custom claiming the force of law; his conclusion was that customs that were unreasonable were not law. Coke, on the other hand, was deciding a case in which a royal charter and parliamentary statutes expressly gave a party authority to impose a fine and keep part of it. In addition, the party in question was not a person, an individual lord defending his demesne, but a corporate body

---

Constitution; ever after, *Marbury* has been understood to refer to testing a law against the written text.

[15]8 Co. Rep. 118b, 77 Eng. Rep. 654. The "manor of D.," more fully the "manor of Dale," was a fictional estate used in legal examples much as "Blackacre" is used in modern law school classes.

enforcing professional discipline. The law in this case was not merely the product of custom but had been solemnly adopted by the highest political powers in the state; furthermore, it instituted a seemingly cost-effective and efficient system of enforcement. Could the common law invalidate such an act of Parliament? Coke certainly said that it could.

Historians and lawyers have debated for years whether Coke really meant what he said, whether he really meant to assert the power of the common law to "control" acts of Parliament and declare them "void."[16] It may be that he was merely applying his own rigorous rules for reading poorly drafted statutes,[17] although even in that case he would be defending the common law against legislative meddling; but there is also evidence that he deliberately seized the opportunity to make a constitutional claim, expanding in print what he had said in court.[18] Coke's learned successors certainly thought he was making a more general point. Sir Henry Hobart, who followed Coke at Common Pleas, soon echoed his dictum, declaring that "an Act of Parliament,

[16]See John V. Orth, "Did Sir Edward Coke Mean What He Said?" *Constitutional Commentary* 16 (1999): 33–38.

[17]See Samuel Thorne, "Dr. Bonham's Case," *Law Quarterly Review* 54 (1938): 543–52, and J. W. Gough, *Fundamental Law in English Constitutional History* (Oxford: Clarendon Press, 1955), 31–39.

[18]Charles M. Gray, "Bonham's Case Reviewed," *Proceedings of the American Philosophical Society* 116 (1972): 35–58. Coke repeated himself in 1612 in *Rowles v. Mason,* 2 Brownl. & Golds. 192, 198, 123 Eng. Rep. 892, 895 (C.P. 1612).

made against natural equity, as to make a man a Judge in his own case, is void in itself, for *jura naturae sunt immutabilia* [the laws of nature are unchangeable], and they are *leges legum* [the laws of law]."[19] And a century later Sir John Holt, chief justice of the Court of King's Bench, labeled Coke's dictum "far from any extravagancy," "a very reasonable and true saying."[20]

Why Coke might have wanted to make so momentous a statement at that particular time requires a word about English political history. When in the early seventeenth century the newly arrived Stuart monarchs made a bid for supreme power, their opponents searched for some counterbalancing English institution. Not unnaturally, Coke, the great lawyer and judge, sought to locate limits on royal power in the common law, that is, as a practical matter, in the courts. According to his own account, Coke had told King James only two years earlier that even a king was unfit to judge a case between himself and his subjects. An Englishman's life and property, Coke said, were protected by the "artificial reason and judgment of law," and the king himself was "sub Deo et lege" (under God and the law), a concept King James liked no better than King John had

[19]*Day v. Savadge*, Hob. 85, 87, 80 Eng. Rep. 235, 237 (C.P. 1615).

[20]*City of London v. Wood*, 12 Mod. 669, 687, 88 Eng. Rep. 1592, 1603 (K.B. 1701). For a reading of Holt's opinion based on manuscript sources rather than the printed opinion, see Philip A. Hamburger, "Revolution and Judicial Review: Chief Justice Holt's Opinion in City of London v. Wood," *Columbia Law Review* 94 (1994): 2091–2153.

liked Magna Carta four hundred years earlier.[21] Despite the facts that law is normally an instrument of government power, not a restraint on it, and that English judges were royal appointees, at the time still lacking secure tenure, Coke sought to use certain powerful medieval concepts, such as natural law and customary right, to cabin the sovereign; he counted on a cadre of resolute and well-connected judges like himself to stand up to the king.[22] As things turned out, the courts proved to be frail reeds. The only institution that was a match for the Crown was Parliament, as demonstrated on the bloody battlefields of the English Civil War, 1642–1649, and in the Glorious Revolution of 1688.

Sir William Blackstone, writing in the mid-eighteenth century, in the tranquil aftermath of the English constitutional crisis, certainly recognized the implications of Parliament's victory. In the first volume of his famous *Commentaries on the Laws of England* (1765), Blackstone listed ten rules for statutory construction. "Lastly," he put the largely meaningless rule, "acts of parliament that are im-

[21]12 Co. Rep. 65, 77 Eng. Rep. 1343. Although English kings had once actually decided cases, the practice had ceased to be usual by the end of the fifteenth century, and Coke was correctly stating the situation as it had been for generations. See William S. Holdsworth, *A History of English Law,* 7th ed., rev. (London: Methuen, 1956), 1: 194, 207.

[22]At the time Coke spoke and until 1700, English judges held office "durante bene placito" (during good pleasure) and could be removed from office by the king, as Coke himself was. See Catherine Drinker Bowen, *The Lion and the Throne: The Life and Times of Sir Edward Coke* (Boston: Little, Brown, 1956), 370–90.

possible to be performed are of no validity."[23] Blackstone conceded that he knew it was "generally laid down more largely" that "acts of parliament contrary to reason are void." The source of this view was, of course, Sir Edward Coke, who had said just that in *Dr. Bonham's Case:* acts of Parliament are void if "against common right and reason, *or* repugnant, *or* impossible to be performed." But Blackstone thought the old rule anachronistic, even if backed by so high an authority as Coke: "If the parliament will positively enact a thing to be done which is unreasonable," the Commentator candidly conceded, "I know of no power that can control it," giving Coke the lie direct.[24]

To put his meaning beyond all doubt, Blackstone boldly took as his example the very one Coke had used in *Dr. Bonham's Case:* whether a law could make a man a judge in his own case. Blackstone agreed with Coke on the utter undesirability of the practice; elsewhere he described it as a characteristic of life in the state of nature, "one of the evils civil government was intended to remedy."[25] But he was con-

---

[23]Blackstone, *Commentaries,* 1: 91. The classic example of an "impossible" statute was one that purported to "make a woman a man, and a man a woman." See A. V. Dicey, *Introduction to the Study of the Law of the Constitution,* 7th ed. (London: Macmillan, 1908), 41. See also William S. Holdsworth, *A History of English Law* (London: Methuen, 1938), 12: 344 n. 5. Of course, it was never necessary for a law to change the physical characteristics of the sexes, when it was possible to require that for all legal purposes a woman should be treated like a man and vice versa.

[24]Blackstone, *Commentaries,* 1: 91.

[25]Ibid. (1769), 4: 8.

cerned with whether the judicial power could prevent that particular evil. Giving as much scope as he could to Coke's celebrated dictum, Blackstone in the end confined it to cases of unintended consequences: "Thus if an act of parliament gives a man power to try all causes that arise within his manor of Dale; yet, if a cause should arise in which he himself is party, the act is construed not to extend to that; because it is unreasonable that any man should determine his own quarrel."[26] But Blackstone knew he could not leave it at that. In candor, with uncharacteristically awkward words that seemed almost wrung from him, he haltingly continued: "If we could conceive it possible for the parliament to enact, that he should try as well his own causes as those of other persons, there is no court that has power to defeat the intention of the legislature, when couched in such evident and express words, as leave no doubt whether it was the intent of the legislature or no."[27] Refusing to the end to concede the rightfulness, even the lawfulness, of the proceeding, Blackstone rested the result in this case on power alone: no English court has the power to declare an act of Parliament void.[28]

Power, not process, was the heart of the matter. Blackstone

[26]Ibid. (1765), 1: 91.

[27]Ibid.

[28]Parliament itself showed a commendable sensitivity to the need to provide disinterested justice. See, e.g., 17 Geo. 3, c. 55, § 6 (1777) (disqualifying justices of the peace who were also master hatters from exercising jurisdiction over labor disputes in the hat-making trade); 39 & 40 Geo. 3,

was by no means indifferent to the demands of due process, when the courts had power to act. In their supervision of the justices of the peace, for example, the common law courts had insisted on proper procedures. As Blackstone rather waspishly put it: "The courts of common law have thrown in one check upon them, by making it necessary to *summon* the party accused before he is condemned."[29] Earlier in his *Commentaries* Blackstone had had no hesitation citing Littleton to the effect that a custom had to meet the test of reason if it were to be given the force of law,[30] but by Blackstone's day it seemed obvious that custom and legislation had to be measured by different legal yardsticks. Custom was obviously subject to the approval of the common law judges; they alone determined whether it had produced a rule that had become legally enforceable. But if applied to acts of Parliament, judicial review, Blackstone thought, would "set the judicial power above that of the legislature, which would be subversive of all government."[31] Palliate it as he might, the result is not pretty. Parliament can do anything, even so egregious a thing as make a man a judge in his own case.

---

c. 106, § 16 (Combination Act, 1800) (disqualifying justices of the peace who were also employers from exercising jurisdiction over labor disputes in their own industry); 6 Geo. 4, c. 129, § 13 (1825) (same). See also John V. Orth, *Combination and Conspiracy: A Legal History of Trade Unionism, 1721–1906* (Oxford: Clarendon Press, 1991), 19, 50, 52, 81, 90.

[29]William Blackstone, *Commentaries on the Laws of England* (Oxford, 1769), 4: 279 (italics in original).

[30]Ibid., 1: 77.

[31]Ibid. 91.

Coke had been defending not only Dr. Bonham's right to a fair trial but also the law's supremacy over the powers that be. In later years it would be possible to minimize Coke's contribution in *Dr. Bonham's Case* as mere insistence on strict rules of statutory construction. At most he could be credited with a vain attempt to establish judicial review, later dismissed by Lord Campbell as "a foolish doctrine alleged to have been laid down extra-judicially in Dr. Bonham's Case . . . , a conundrum [that] ought to have been laughed at."[32] But in fact Coke was trying to give content to the law's restraint on power; that is, he was trying to give substance to due process. There were, he thought, things that the supreme power in the state, even the king in Parliament, could not lawfully do, no matter how hard he tried. Limiting how the king could proceed limited to a degree what he could do as well; if the king had to proceed according to the "law of the land," then he could not act arbitrarily, excessively, or without consultation. The king, and Parliament too, should be "under God and the law."

Coke probably thought he had found the perfect example, one on which all could agree: the procedural horror of making a man a judge in his own case. The common law, he thought, would certainly void a statute so contrary to "common right and reason." But he had earlier lectured King

[32]Lord Campbell, *The Lives of the Chief Justices of England* (1849; reprint, London, 1873), 1: 298. Risible or not, Lord Campbell admitted that he had "often" heard it "quoted in parliament against the binding obligation of obnoxious statutes" (ibid.).

James against assaults on property as well, the substantive horror that came to be exemplified by the case of "taking from A and giving to B." An Englishman's property, Coke had told the king, was protected by the "artificial reason and judgment of law," a concept better known today as due process. As English history unfolded, Coke's fears could be dismissed as at best eccentric, at worst a joke. Parliament was supreme; it had won the war. Fearful of executive power, it had acted promptly to guarantee judicial independence,[33] but English courts were not expected to review statutes for their reasonableness, an increasingly nebulous concept. Firmly in the hands of propertied classes suspicious of central power, Parliament in any event was unlikely to violate the rights of property. But the parliamentary supremacy Blackstone so reluctantly recognized in 1760 was within a few years to lead to a new war, the American War of Independence, spawning a new nation and grafting a new and vigorous branch onto the common law tradition.

In England, the land whose law gave content to the phrase "the law of the land" and the nation where the demand for "due process of law" was first sounded, the great

[33]The Act of Settlement, 12 & 13 Wm. 3, c. 2, § 3 (1700), established a new standard for judicial tenure, "quamdiu se bene gesserit" (so long as he shall behave himself well). The U.S. Constitution, Article 3, § 1, translating from the Latin, provides that federal judges hold their offices "during good Behaviour," the legal code words for lifetime tenure. For a critical analysis of English practice since 1880, see Robert Stevens, *The Independence of the Judiciary: The View from the Lord Chancellor's Office* (Oxford: Clarendon Press, 1993).

phrases failed to retain their vitality; instead, the vaguer bounds of public opinion and the "rule of law" had to be relied on to limit government power.[34] In the newly constituted United States of America, by contrast, both state and federal constitutions expressly guaranteed "due process of law" (or, what came to the same thing, "the law of the land"), keeping both phrases evergreen. Consistent with such strictures, could a man be made a judge in his own case? In the abstract, probably not, although for a century and a half a substantial number of American states allowed something very like it with respect to the lowest level of the judiciary, paying the salaries of magistrates or justices of the peace from the fines they levied. In its way, the practice was arguably worse than the disciplinary procedures of the Royal College of Physicians because the American decision maker personally pocketed the proceeds of justice; the Royal College merely put the money in its corporate treasury. But at the time it probably seemed a reasonable way of keeping

---

[34]The "rule of law" has been defined as "a concept of the utmost importance but having no defined, nor readily definable, content." See David M. Walker, *The Oxford Companion to Law* (New York: Oxford University Press, 1980), 1093. In the English legal tradition, "the rule of law" is intimately tied up with the scholarship of Professor A. V. Dicey, whose magisterial book *Introduction to the Study of the Law of the Constitution* (London, 1885, and later editions) popularized the phrase. See Richard A. Cosgrove, *The Rule of Law: Albert Venn Dicey, Victorian Jurist* (London: Macmillan, 1980). See also the book review by John V. Orth, "On the Relation Between the Rule of Law and Public Opinion," *Michigan Law Review* 80 (1982): 753–64.

down the cost of government and encouraging vigilance by providing "payment by results." It was not until 1928, in a particularly egregious case, that the U.S. Supreme Court finally declared the practice, however long-continued, unconstitutional. Citing *Dr. Bonham's Case,* the Court relied on Coke's reasoning: for a case to be decided by a judge with "a direct, substantial, pecuniary interest" in its outcome, said Chief Justice William Howard Taft, is a violation of due process.[35]

By the early twentieth century, the practice of judicial review in America, while contentious in specific applications, was nonetheless firmly established as a general principle. The judge in his own case posed a rather obvious problem of procedure, or, if you will, of "procedural due process." By this time, however, there was also another kind of problem involving due process, the A-to-B problem, that came eventually to be known by the curious name of "substantive due process."[36]

[35] *Tumey v. Ohio,* 273 U.S. 510, 523 (1928). Some state constitutions today expressly prohibit the practice; see, e.g., North Carolina Constitution, Art. 4, § 21: "In no case shall the compensation of any Judge or Magistrate be dependent upon his decision or upon the collection of costs." See John V. Orth, *The North Carolina State Constitution: A Reference Guide* (Westport, Conn.: Greenwood Press, 1993), 117–18.

[36] The phrase "substantive due process" was first used by a U.S. Supreme Court justice in 1948. See Wayne McCormack, "Economic Substantive Due Process and the Right of Livelihood," *Kentucky Law Journal* 82 (1993): 397, 406–7, citing *Republic Natural Gas Co. v. Oklahoma,* 334 U.S. 62, 90 (1948) (Rutledge, J., dissenting).

3

Case II. Taking from A and Giving to B: The Ambiguous Paradigm

An act of the legislature (for I cannot call it a law) contrary to the
first great principles of the social compact, cannot be considered a
rightful exercise of legislative authority. The obligation of a law in
governments established on express compact, and of republican
principles, must be determined by the nature of the power, on which
it is founded. A few instances will suffice to explain what I mean. A
law that punished a citizen for an innocent action, or, in other
words, for an act, which, when done, was in violation of no existing
law; a law that destroys, or impairs, the lawful private contracts of
citizens; a law that makes a man a Judge in his own cause; or a law
that takes property from A and gives it to B: It is against all reason
and justice, for a people to entrust a Legislature with such powers;
and, therefore, it cannot be presumed that they have done it.

SAMUEL CHASE, J. (1798)

In the first reported opinion of the U.S. Supreme Court
that mentions the hoary problem of making a man a

judge in his own case, *Calder v. Bull,*[1] Justice Samuel Chase also enumerated other situations that in his opinion were just as egregious, last among them "a law that takes property from A and gives it to B," an example that would have a long and curious career.[2] Before it is finally consigned to the dustbin of musty maxims almost a century and a half later, the A-to-B paradigm will cause a great expansion of judicial power and even precipitate a major constitutional crisis. Chase began, however, with easier cases.

First, he instanced "a law that punished a citizen for an innocent action, or, in other words, for an act, which, when

[1] 3 U.S. (3 Dall.) 386, 388 (1798). Reference to the abuse of making a man a judge in his own case actually appears ten years earlier, in the very first volume of the U.S. Reports but not in a Supreme Court case. In litigation in the Common Pleas Court of Philadelphia County an attorney had argued, "Surely the Legislature could not mean to make a man the judge both of fact and law in his own cause" and cited Chief Justice Holt. See *Penman v. Wayne,* 1 U.S. (1 Dall.) 241, 243–44 (Pa. Com. Pl., Phila. Co. 1788).

[2] As every law student quickly learns, property lawyers regularly use letters of the alphabet to designate parties to property transactions; the usage is deeply rooted in the common law and predates the American Revolution. See, e.g., William Blackstone, *Commentaries on the Laws of England* (Oxford, 1766), 2: 180: "If an estate be granted to A and B and their heirs, this makes them immediately joint tenants in the lands." See also John V. Orth, "Joint Tenancies," in *Thompson on Real Property,* ed. David Thomas (Charlottesville, Va.: Michie, 1994), 4: 9–11. In the same way, property lawyers to this day use the mythical estate of "Blackacre" to stand for the subject of property transactions; Coke and Blackstone used the "manor of Dale" for the same purpose. In all cases the object is the same, to abstract from particular names and places and focus on the essence of what is done.

done, was in violation of no existing law," what is usually referred to as an *ex post facto* law. The common law in the eighteenth century had slowly begun to confront the issue of retrospective laws as the pace of legislation increased and the rational methods of the Enlightenment spread to the study of English law.[3] Radical thinkers quickly recognized that the common law itself appeared to be nothing but a vast collection of *ex post facto* laws. Jeremy Bentham cynically observed, "The common law is made by the judges on the same principle as a man makes laws for his dog—he waits till the dog has done something he does not like and then punishes him for it."[4] The root of the problem lay in the barely acknowledged fact of the gradual breakdown of the medieval consensus on the existence and content of natural law.

When Sir Edward Coke, and Sir Thomas Littleton before him, invoked reason as the sovereign test of lawfulness, they had assumed that judges, masters of the "artificial reason" of the law, would by and large agree on what legal reason required, or at least on what it forbade.[5] But in the eighteenth

[3]See, e.g., William Blackstone, *Commentaries on the Laws of England* (Oxford, 1765), 1: 46.

[4]Jeremy Bentham, "The Truth Versus Ashhurst," in *Works of Jeremy Bentham*, ed. John Bowring (London, 1843), 5: 235–36. See also John Austin, *Lectures on Jurisprudence*, ed. Robert Campbell, 3d ed. (London, 1863), 2: 671–82.

[5]See John V. Orth, "How Many Judges Does It Take to Make a Supreme Court?" *Constitutional Commentary*, forthcoming, pointing out that for seven hundred years the common law courts had four judges apiece, implying a belief that tie votes were unlikely.

century, reason began slowly to turn in on itself. If right and, more important, wrong were not obvious to all right-thinking persons, at least in most cases, then common law judgments could come, as it were, as a surprise; judicial decisions could appear to be based on rules developed after the fact. This fundamental problem with the origin of the common law was never solved; it was simply ignored because the common law by that time was so old that its rules in the vast majority of cases could plausibly be described as promulgated before the fact, *ex ante*. In the rare cases not so provided for, natural law in some attenuated sense still governed.[6]

Where statutes, which after all have always been recognized as making new law, were concerned, the unfairness of retrospective application was obvious; so unanimous was its condemnation at the time of the formation of the federal union that the U.S. Constitution categorically prohibited both the national government and the states from adopting such legislation: "No . . . *ex post facto* Law shall be passed,"[7] that is, passed by Congress, and "no state shall . . . pass any . . . *ex post facto* law."[8] The very case in which Chase compiled his catalog of horrors required the Supreme Court for the first time to interpret the *ex post facto* clause. Did it apply to all laws or only to laws imposing punishments, that is,

[6]See Benjamin N. Cardozo, *The Nature of the Judicial Process* (New Haven: Yale University Press, 1921), 142.

[7]U.S. Constitution, Art. 1, § 9.

[8]Ibid., § 10.

to criminal laws? Drawing inspiration from the state constitutions, many of which were more explicit on the point,[9] the Court concluded that the clause banned only *ex post facto* criminal laws, laws which (in Chase's terms) dealt out punishments for acts, which when done violated no existing law.

Second, Chase named "a law that destroys, or impairs, the lawful private contracts of citizens." This refers to state interference with private agreements, usually arising in a commercial context. Prior to the eighteenth century, contract did not play a very large role in common law thinking, which was historically centered on property, particularly property in land.[10] Blackstone notably ignored the subject, devoting an entire volume to land law and barely thirty pages to contract. In England the advance of trade, particularly international trade, spurred the development of con-

[9]See, e.g., North Carolina Constitution of 1776, Declaration of Rights, § 24: "That retrospective laws, punishing acts committed before the existence of such laws, and by them only declared criminal, are oppressive, unjust, and incompatible with liberty; wherefore, no *ex post facto* law ought to be made." The Maryland Constitution was almost identical (Md. Const. of 1776, Decl. of Rights, § 15), and the Massachusetts Constitution was to the same effect (Mass. Const. of 1780, Decl. of Rights, § 24). Chase cited them all in *Calder*, 3 U.S. (3 Dall.), at 391–92. In substantially similar form, the same provision appears in the most recent North Carolina Constitution (N.C. Const., Art. 1, § 16). See John V. Orth, *The North Carolina State Constitution: A Reference Guide* (Westport, Conn.: Greenwood Press, 1993), 52–53.

[10]See John V. Orth, "Contract and the Common Law," in *The State and Freedom of Contract*, ed. Harry N. Scheiber (Stanford: Stanford University Press, 1998), 44–65.

tract law and related legal doctrines, as seen in the landmark decisions of Lord Mansfield, chief justice of King's Bench from 1756 to 1788.[11] In America the experience with land speculation, depreciating currencies, default on government debt, and legislative rescues of impecunious debtors convinced many in the founding generation of the imperative need for the protection of private agreements. Here again the U.S. Constitution spoke unequivocally: "No state shall . . . pass any . . . law impairing the obligation of contracts,"[12] a precocious recognition of the large role contract was to play in economic development.

Next, Chase recited the hoary problem of "a law that makes a man a Judge in his own cause." In this regard there was no specific constitutional reference; nowhere did the federal Constitution or Bill of Rights require in so many words an impartial judge. Perhaps the jury was expected to screen the defendant,[13] or perhaps it was left to the state constitutions. More likely, Coke and his collaborators had made anything else seem so obviously wrong that it did not require express mention: it simply lay too deep for words,

[11]See Charles A. Bane, "From Holt and Mansfield to Story to Llewellyn and Mentschikoff: The Progressive Development of Commercial Law," *University of Miami Law Review* 37 (1983): 351–77.

[12]U.S. Constitution, Art. 1, § 10. Possibly reflecting the view that contract law was peculiarly the province of state legislation, the Constitution contains no comparable restriction on congressional legislation.

[13]See ibid., Sixth Amendment: "In all criminal prosecutions, the accused shall enjoy the right to a speedy and public trial, by an impartial jury."

whatever Blackstone had lately said. When a question concerning the need for judicial impartiality did arise, it was
answered by reference to the requirement in state and federal constitutions that no person be deprived of life, liberty,
or property "without due process of law" (or against the "law
of the land").[14]

It is an interesting question of hypothetical history,
whether the due process clause could have been pressed into
service in the prior cases as well, had the Federal Constitution not included an express *ex post facto* clause or contracts
clause. In other words, would the constitutional requirement of due process have been enough, by itself, to preclude
laws punishing acts not criminal when committed or laws
impairing the obligation of contracts? Possibly.[15] Chase cer-

[14]*Tumey v. Ohio*, 273 U.S. 510, 523 (1928). Some state constitutions today expressly prohibit the practice. See, e.g., North Carolina Constitution, Art. 4, § 21: "In no case shall the compensation of any Judge or
Magistrate be dependent upon his decision or upon the collection of
costs." See also Orth, *The North Carolina State Constitution*, 117–18.

[15]One scholar has described the due process clauses as, after the *ex
post facto* clause and the contracts clause, "the *third* guaranty against
retroactivity of legislation." See Frank R. Strong, *Substantive Due Process
of Law: A Dichotomy of Sense and Nonsense* (Durham, N.C.: Carolina
Academic Press, 1986), 30 n. 5 (italics in original). As to the contracts
question, history eventually provided an answer. See *Allied Structural
Steel Co. v. Spannaus*, 438 U.S. 234, 241 ("the Contract Clause receded
into comparative desuetude with the adoption of the Fourteenth
Amendment [in 1868], and particularly with the development of the
large body of jurisprudence under the Due Process Clause of that
Amendment").

tainly thought that no specific prohibitions were required to ban any of the cases he listed. And later courts agreed that, insofar as the judge in his own case was concerned, general terms incorporating some at least of the "first great principles of the social compact" were good enough.

Finally, after this catalog of old (and fairly simple) problems, Chase reached the new and portentous one: "a law that takes property from A and gives it to B." Here again there was no clear constitutional reference. The Constitution as originally adopted did not address the issue at all, but the Fifth Amendment contained two clauses that were arguably relevant, at least insofar as federal law was concerned, the due process clause and the adjacent takings clause: "No person shall . . . be deprived of life, liberty, or property, without due process of law; nor shall private property be taken for public use without just compensation."

What exactly is wrong with a law that takes A's property and gives it to B? The word "takes" obviously suggests the takings clause, concerning the state's taking of private property for public purposes, that is, the sovereign power of condemnation or eminent domain. If that is the reference, then the problem with taking from A and giving to B lies not in what is said but in what is left unsaid: the problem is not the taking itself but something else. If the state invokes its power to take the property of A for the use of someone other than the public—if B in the equation is not the state but another private party—then the problem is the misuse of public power for private gain.[16] (In the modern world, as we will see, a "public use" may even include turning the property over to a private person.[17]) Or, if the state takes A's property for public use but does not pay A just compensation, then the case is one of simple expropriation.[18]

The problem with taking the property of A and giving it to B may lie elsewhere, however, as the use to which the maxim was put in American constitutional history will amply demonstrate. The key word in the early cases may in fact be "property" rather than "taking." Here again the problem seems to lie in what is left unsaid; the problem may be that no property of A may be taken, for B's use or for anyone (or no one) else's use, "without due process of law." Viewed in this light, the property aspect of the due process clause is intended to protect certain rights from interference by arbitrary legislation. In later years, in place of property other interests came to be substituted, such as liberty (or freedom) of contract or the right of privacy. By then, the problem had be-

[16]For the historical background, see Buckner F. Melton Jr., "Eminent Domain, 'Public Use,' and the Conundrum of Original Intent," *Natural Resources Journal* 36 (1996): 59–85.

[17]*Hawaii Housing Authority v. Midkiff,* 467 U.S. 229 (1984), discussed in chapter 6.

[18]This was the issue in two earlier cases raising the A-to-B problem: *Bowman v. Middleton,* 1 Bay. 252 (S.C. 1792), and *Van Horne's Lessee v. Dorrance,* 2 U.S. (2 Dall.) 304 (Cir. Ct. Pa., 1794). On the history of the takings clause, see James W. Ely Jr., "'That Due Satisfaction May Be Made': The Fifth Amendment and the Origins of the Compensation Principle," *American Journal of Legal History* 36 (1992): 1–18.

come that nothing of A's could be taken without due process. In this case, the emphasis is not on the absence of "public use" or "just compensation," as in the takings cases properly so called, but on the bare taking (or deprivation) itself.[19]

Chase's invocation of "reason and justice," although reminiscent of Littleton and Coke, did not go unchallenged. Justice James Iredell in reply denied that judges can be guided by so uncertain a rule: "The ideas of natural justice are regulated by no fixed standard: the ablest and the purest men have differed upon the subject."[20] Long reasoning had made reason itself an uncertain guide, but Americans no longer needed to rely only on the "artificial reason" of the common law to protect life, liberty, and property. As Iredell foresaw, the existence of a written constitution implied a judicial approach to constitutional decision making that began with the text, a supposedly "fixed standard," rather than with vague "first principles," however great.[21] Just as Blackstone reined in the judicial exuberance of Coke, so Iredell cautioned Chase, and just as Coke was ultimately defeated

[19]One scholar, who has seemingly reviewed all the due process cases, reports that until recently the Supreme Court has not troubled to limit the word "taking" to the cases arising under the takings clause and "deprivation" to cases under the due process clause. See Strong, *Substantive Due Process of Law*, 202 n. 414.

[20]*Calder v. Bull*, 3 U.S. (3 Dall.), at 388.

[21]A decade earlier Iredell had still thought there was some room for natural law in judicial decision making. In a private letter he wrote, "Without an express Constitution the powers of the Legislature would undoubtedly have been absolute (as the Parliament in Great Britain is

by the development of the English constitution, so Chase was limited by the fact of an "express compact." But American textualism was not to prove so confining as English power politics: the inclusion in state and federal constitutions of Coke's favorite legal phrase, "due process of law," meant that American judges were eventually able to apply many natural law principles as well as some of their own personal predilections. As American legal scholars delight in observing, Iredell's views triumphed only in form; "in substance, however, the beliefs of Justice Chase have prevailed as the Court continually has expanded its basis for reviewing the acts of other branches of government."[22]

The dialogue between Chase and Iredell in 1798 seemed to assume the power of judicial review, the power to declare whether a law was valid or void; other decisions made during the Supreme Court's first decade seemed to proceed from the same premise.[23] But the plainest statement of the doctrine was made five years later in 1803 in *Marbury v. Madison*, the case ever after cited for the proposition that in

---

held to be), and any act passed, *not inconsistent with natural justice* (for the curb is avowed by the judges even in England), would have been binding on the people." See Griffith J. McRee, *Life and Correspondence of James Iredell* (New York, 1858), 2: 172 (italics in original).

[22]John E. Nowak et al., *Constitutional Law,* 2d ed. (St. Paul, Minn.: West Publishing Company, 1983), 426.

[23]See David P. Currie, *The Constitution in the Supreme Court: The First Hundred Years, 1789–1888* (Chicago: University of Chicago Press, 1985), 6–9, 20–23, 29–30, 37–41, 51–54.

America courts determine the validity of laws, including acts of the legislature.[24] *Marbury* involved the claim of a political appointee deprived of his office by a new administration and was part of the high politics of its day.[25] Technically, the deciding question was whether an act of Congress gave the Supreme Court jurisdiction to hear the case. To answer that question, Chief Justice John Marshall on behalf of the Court tested the statute against the Constitution and found it wanting, restating in the process Coke's dictum in American terms. Whereas Coke had declared "void" an act of Parliament that was "against common right and reason," Marshall echoed Iredell and substituted for an appeal to reason an appeal to the U.S. Constitution: "A law repugnant to the constitution is void."[26] In America the courts would determine the validity of all law, whether customary or statutory; in England, the homeland of the common law, the courts lacked the power to invalidate statutes.

Whether a law that takes property from A and gives it to B could pass muster in the courts of the United States would depend in the final analysis not on reason or first

[24]5 U.S. (1 Cranch) 137 (1803).

[25]For a discussion of the politics of *Marbury*, see John V. Orth, *The Judicial Power of the United States: The Eleventh Amendment in American History* (New York: Oxford University Press, 1987), 31–34.

[26]5 U.S. (1 Cranch) 180.

principles but on the Constitution and the judges who construed it. How the A-to-B problem might materialize was
hypothesized by Justice Joseph Story in 1829 in *Wilkinson v.
Leland*.[27] In the actual facts of that case, Rhode Island had
passed a law purporting to confirm Wilkinson's title to certain land in the state. The land in question had belonged to
a citizen of New Hampshire who had died and whose ex-
ecutor had sold it pursuant to dubious authority from a New
Hampshire court. Because the U.S. Supreme Court found
that the title was valid without regard to the Rhode Island
legislation, it did not need to decide the question of the
constitutionality of the statute. In extensive dicta Story
nonetheless examined the question of whether legislation
could change the existing title to land, taking it from A and
giving it to B. In one sense the potential problem involved
retrospective legislation[28] and, had the *ex post facto* clause
not been limited to criminal laws (by the decision in *Calder
v. Bull*), could have been addressed in those terms. Lacking
that purchase on the issue, Story addressed the problem as
one involving a legislative taking of private property: "We
know of no case, in which a legislative act to transfer the
property of A to B without his consent, has ever been held

[27]27 U.S. (2 Pet.) 627 (1829).
[28]See James Kent, *Commentaries on American Law,* ed. O. W. Holmes,
12th ed. (Boston, 1873), 1: 455, who cites *Wilkinson* in support of the
proposition that "a retrospective statute, affecting and changing vested
rights, is very generally considered, in this country, as founded on unconstitutional principles, and consequently inoperative and void."

a constitutional exercise of legislative power in any state in the Union."[29]

Another way of looking at the question discussed by Story would have been to see it as a question concerning separation of powers and the proper distinction between legislative and judicial roles. A statute like the Rhode Island law could be thought of as taking A's property, yet a judicial decision like the Supreme Court's ruling was merely a declaration of B's rightful ownership.[30] Could a statute reverse a judicial decision? (Actually, the Rhode Island legislation had attempted to *affirm* a judicial decision, but if it could effectively do that, it could do the other as well.) In fact, in a somewhat earlier North Carolina case involving a legislative attempt to alter title to property, the state's highest court had voided the statute on the ground that it violated a state constitutional provision declaring the legislative, executive, and judicial powers "forever separate and distinct."[31] The federal Constitution, although it also separates power, lacks

[29]27 U.S. (2 Pet.) 627, 658 (1829).

[30]Latterly it has been suggested, even in the highest judicial circles, that there may be such a thing as a "judicial taking." See *Stevens v. Cannon Beach,* 510 U.S. 1207 (1994) (Scalia, J., dissenting from the denial of a petition for a writ of certiorari), cited in chapter 6.

[31]*Robinson v. Barfield,* 6 N.C. 391 (1818) (construing N.C. Const. of 1776, Decl. of Rts., § 4). The separation of powers provision appears today in the North Carolina Constitution, Art. 1, § 6. See Orth, *The North Carolina State Constitution,* 41–44. For a modern application of the provision, see John V. Orth, "'Forever Separate and Distinct': Separation of Powers in North Carolina," *North Carolina Law Review* 59 (1983): 1–28.

an express separation of powers clause, so Story was denied that purchase on the issue as well.

Chancellor James Kent, a contemporary of Story and author of the influential *Commentaries on American Law,* shared the justice's abhorrence of taking from A and giving to B, but he still understood the problem to be as much a takings problem as a due process problem. Citing *Wilkinson,* he wrote: "It undoubtedly must rest, as a general rule, in the wisdom of the legislature, to determine when public uses require the assumption of private property; but if they should take it for a purpose not of a public nature, as if the legislature should take the property of A and give it to B, or if they should vacate a grant of property, or of a franchise, under the pretext of some public use or service, such cases would be gross abuses of their discretion, and fraudulent attacks on private right, and the law would be clearly unconstitutional and void."[32] Kent thus tried to wrestle the A-to-B problem into a question of whether the transfer (or extinction) of a property right served a genuine public purpose. If it did, the focus would then shift to the calculation of the necessary compensation—as indeed it still does in takings cases. But if the taking was not for a public purpose, Kent knew it was wrong, a "gross abuse of discretion," a "fraudulent attack on private right," "clearly unconstitutional and void," although like Justice Story he apparently saw no need to put his finger on a specific clause. Such a taking could not possibly be

[32]Kent, *Commentaries,* 2: 340.

constitutional; for want of a better phrase, it could be described as a violation of "due process of law."[33] The way ahead, in cases not invoking the sovereign power of condemnation, involved an ever greater concentration on the requirements of due process, which if not satisfied could not be rectified by a simple compensatory payment. Life, liberty, and (what is most important to the present inquiry) property could not be taken without due process. With due process, money need not be involved; without it, no cash payment, however large, would be enough.

Wilkinson indicated that legislation could not constitutionally "transfer the property of A to B," but the particular statute operated in a context of adjudication; that is, the legislature had attempted to resolve a dispute over the ownership of land. Just as Sir Edward Coke years earlier had admonished King James that an Englishman's property was protected by the "artificial reason of the law" and that the king himself could not exercise judicial power, so Justice Story reminded the states that the courts were the proper bodies to try titles. The attempted exercise of that power by another branch of government could be described as a pro-

[33]Since federal law was not involved in *Wilkinson,* the due process clause of the Fifth Amendment was not at issue, and since the Fourteenth Amendment, which limits state action, had not yet been adopted, it was not involved either; so Story must have been referring to Rhode Island law. Since Rhode Island had not adopted a constitution after Independence but still relied on its colonial charter, Story probably was going directly to Magna Carta, most likely mediated through Sir Edward Coke.

cedural violation: just as a man could not be made a judge in his own case, so one who was not a judge could not make judicial rulings.[34] A half century later, Justice Samuel Miller repeated the lesson in *Davidson v. New Orleans,* although this time outside an explicit adjudicative context: "A statute which declares in terms, and without more, that the full and exclusive title of a described piece of land, which is now in A, shall be and hereby is vested in B, would, if effectual, deprive A of his property without due process of law."[35] The A-to-B paradigm had by then become detached from the procedural context and was ready for more general service.

Making a man a judge in his own case was the standard illustration of a violation of natural justice. It was for centuries (and remains) a prime example of a violation of due process. When, in the late eighteenth century, it was reinforced as an exemplar (or a paradigm) with taking from A and giving to B, there was at first no conscious change: this, too, would violate due process, if a judicial proceeding was denied. But under cover of the phrase "taking from A and giving to B" another meaning lurked, redistributive and substantive. When in the late nineteenth century regulatory legislation threatened vested interests and individual entrepreneurship, due process jurisprudence already contained

[34]See Wallace Mendelson, "A Missing Link in the Evolution of Due Process," *Vanderbilt Law Review* 10 (1956): 125–37, who describes the "separation of powers ideas" as the missing link in the transition from procedural to substantive due process.

[35]96 U.S. 97, 102 (1878).

the germ of a response. Taking from A and giving to B could do double duty, illustrating both a procedural and a substantive violation. Legislative takings could plausibly be seen in contexts other than adjudication; much regulatory legislation could be comprehended under the same A-to-B paradigm. As substantive due process emerged as a new legal category, taking from A and giving to B became the prime example of what it forbade, and eventually under its cover an even simpler and starker paradigm would emerge, "taking from A," that comprehended even more legislation.

4

Case II Continued. Taking from A and Giving to B: Economic Substantive Due Process

If it is competent to impose upon an employer, who has omitted no legal duty and has committed no wrong, a liability based solely upon a legislative fiat that his business is inherently dangerous, it is equally competent to fix upon him a special tax for the support of hospitals and other charitable institutions, upon the theory that they are devoted largely to the alleviation of ills primarily due to his business. In its final and simple analysis that is taking the property of A and giving it to B, and that cannot be done under our Constitutions.

WILLIAM E. WERNER, J. (1911)

From its original use to encapsulate what was wrong with legislative interference with individual titles, the paradigm case of taking from A and giving to B became in the heyday of laissez-faire a powerful rhetorical weapon against regulatory legislation. In a notorious 1911 decision invalidating New York's pioneering Workmen's Compensation Act, *Ives v. South Buffalo Railway Co.*,[1] the state's high-est court used the phrase to clinch the case against the statute under both state and federal constitutions. Describ-ing the act's "central and controlling feature" to be that "the employer is responsible to the employee for every accident in the course of employment, whether the employer is at fault or not, and whether the employee is at fault or not," the court denounced it as "plainly revolutionary."[2] In a du-bious excursion into legal history, the judges declared: "When our Constitutions were adopted, it was the law of the land that no man who was without fault or negligence could be held liable in damages for injuries sustained by an-other."[3] To change that principle by imposing "upon an em-ployer, who has omitted no legal duty and has committed

194 N.E. 431 (N.Y. 1911). By contrast, the Washington and Wisconsin courts held that comparable acts adopted by their states did not violate due process; see *State ex rel. Davis-Smith Co. v. Clausen*, 117 P. 1101 (Wash. 1911), and *Borgnis v. Falk Co.*, 133 N.W. 209 (Wisc. 1911).

[2]94 N.E. at 436.

[3]Ibid. at 439. It is generally believed that fault was not necessarily a prerequisite to tort liability in the late eighteenth century, at the time of the adoption of the Fifth Amendment to the federal Constitution and the first New York State Constitution, which contained a "law of the land" clause. See G. Edward White, *Tort Law in America: An Intellectual History* (New York: Oxford University Press, 1985), 15–16. But it was cer-tainly becoming central by the time of the adoption of the Fourteenth Amendment in 1868 and was viewed as a near essential in 1894 when the relevant New York Constitution was adopted, by which time a standard due process clause had been added. On the New York Constitution, see Peter J. Galie, *The New York State Constitution: A Reference Guide* (New York: Greenwood Press, 1991), 47–51; within a few years of the decision in

no wrong, a liability based solely upon a legislative fiat . . . is taking the property of A and giving it to B, and that cannot be done under our Constitutions."[4]

At the time *Ives* was decided, the judiciary placed a high value on the maxim, "no liability without fault." It was a judicial commonplace that title to property could not be lost except by the owner's voluntary act or by operation of law.[5] Sales were obviously voluntary transfers, as were gifts, whether during life or at death by means of a will. Involuntary transfers of title occurred by operation of law in the case of criminal fines or penalties or in civil actions in the form of damages, but in either case the property owner could generally be said to have been at fault by violating a

---

Ives, the New York Constitution was amended and a new Workmen's Compensation Act adopted (see 66). The law's constitutionality under the federal Constitution was subsequently upheld by the U.S. Supreme Court (*New York Central Railroad v. White,* 243 U.S. 188 [1917]). For the historical context, see Lawrence M. Friedman and Jack Ladinsky, "Social Change and the Law of Industrial Accidents," *Columbia Law Review* 67 (1967): 50–82. Although originally styled "workmen's compensation," the system has now generally been recharacterized as "worker's compensation"; see, e.g., N.C. Sess. Laws 1979, c. 714, § 1.

[4] 94 N.E., at 440.

[5] See, e.g., *Wetherbee v. Green,* 22 Mich. 311, 314 (1871) (Cooley, J.) ("a man cannot generally be deprived of his property except by his own voluntary act or by operation of law"). In addition to serving on the Michigan Supreme Court, Thomas M. Cooley was the author of influential treatises, including *The Constitutional Limitations Which Rest upon the Legislative Power of the States* (Boston, 1868) and *The Law of Torts* (Chicago, 1879).

law or committing a civil wrong or tort. Taking from A and giving to B could be justified, if at all, only by showing that A owed B compensation for some wrongdoing, the element found noticeably lacking in the New York statute.

Unlike the unconstitutional legislative transfer hypothesized by Justice Story in *Wilkinson v. Leland* almost one hundred years earlier, the New York legislation was not an attempt to resolve a dispute between two individuals over title to specific property. Nor was it the simple taking of a particular item of property from one person and giving it to another, denounced by Justice Miller in *Davidson v. New Orleans.* Instead, A and B as used by the New York court were not shorthand descriptions of named individuals at all but stood for entire classes: A for the class of employers required to contribute to the workmen's compensation fund, and B for the class of employees entitled to recover from that fund for injuries suffered in the course of employment. But because it was possible to state the facts in the workmen's compensation case in the same A-to-B terms that Story and Miller had used earlier, it was possible to make it appear that all the judges were saying the same thing. The truth is that despite the appearance of continuity the old words had been given new meanings. Much of the development had occurred largely out of sight in the state courts,[6]

[6]See, e.g., *Wynehamer v. People,* 13 N.Y. 378, 391, 394 (1856) (invalidating a state prohibition statute as applied to stock on hand at adoption as akin to taking from A and giving to B). *Wynehamer* has been described as "a new starting place in the history of due process." See Edward S.

but it reached its most notorious fruition in the federal courts.

Because the workmen's compensation system could be viewed as functioning to redistribute money from the employer to the employee, it could plausibly be described as taking from A and giving to B. Less plausibly, the U.S. Supreme Court about the same time found an A-to-B problem with an Arkansas statute dealing with a common occurrence in rural America: livestock killed after straying onto railroad tracks. The law provided that unless within thirty days the railroad paid the owner whatever amount he claimed as compensation for the value of his livestock, the owner could sue the railroad for double damages plus attorney's fees. As construed by the state court, the statute did not require that the amount first demanded be the same as the amount sought in the subsequent lawsuit. The practical effect was that the railroad had to pay the initial demand, however extravagant, or risk a judgment for twice the actual damages after a trial by a local jury, raising the potential for abuse reminiscent of that denounced by Sir Thomas Littleton hundreds of years earlier in the case of cattle straying onto the lord's land: the damages might be a ha'penny but the recovery a hundred pounds, which is "against reason." This time the problem was not seen as the absence of a dis-

---

Corwin, *Liberty Against Government* (Baton Rouge: Louisiana State University Press, 1948), 101–2.

interested decision maker ("making a man a judge in his own case"), although local judges and juries could share a generalized hostility to railroads. Rather, the statute seemed to the Supreme Court to require the decision maker to violate the A-to-B paradigm: "It takes property from one and gives it to another, not because of a breach by the former of a duty to the latter or to the public, but because of a lawful exercise of an undoubted right," the railroad's right to defend itself against unjust claims. "Plainly," the Court concluded, "this cannot be done consistently with due process of law."[7]

Minimum wage legislation, even for vulnerable employees, fared no better. In 1923 in *Adkins v. Children's Hospital*,[8] the U.S. Supreme Court invalidated a federal statute setting minimum wages for women in the District of Columbia because it took from A and gave to B. By then the simple paradigm had achieved a more sophisticated statement: the legislation, the Court said, amounts to "a compulsory exaction from the employer for the support of a partially indigent person, for whose condition there rests upon him no peculiar responsibility, and therefore, in effect, arbitrarily shifts to his

---

[7] *St. Louis, Iron Mountain & Southern Railway Co. v. Wynne*, 224 U.S. 354, 360 (1912). But see *Kansas City Southern Railway Co. v. Anderson*, 233 U.S. 325 (1914) (distinguishing *Wynne* in a case involving the same Arkansas statute).

[8] 261 U.S. 525 (1923). See also *Morehead v. New York ex rel. Tipaldo*, 298 U.S. 587 (1936) (invalidating New York minimum wage law for women and children under the Fourteenth Amendment due process clause).

shoulders a burden which, if it belongs to anybody, belongs to society as a whole."[9] Here again, liability was seemingly imposed without fault. Although the A-to-B paradigm was invoked, the starker paradigm nested within it had clearly emerged. "Freedom of contract is," the Court said, "the general rule and restraint the exception."[10] Taking away that freedom was just as bad as taking something tangible from A and handing it over to B.

Although the A-to-B paradigm with its transactional focus had given due process economic content, the economics of due process had shifted from an emphasis on the transfer implicit in taking and giving and toward an emphasis on the taking part of the formula alone. In the New York workmen's compensation case, the Arkansas cattle case, and the District of Columbia minimum wage case, private parties were involved on each side, and the transaction intended by the statute could be portrayed as a transfer of value from one to the other. But not all regulatory legislation could easily be made to fit the A-to-B paradigm; some simply prohibited certain practices. In his 1927 Columbia University Lectures on the Supreme Court of the United States, Charles Evans Hughes, soon to be its chief justice, made the connection in almost parodic fashion. After stating the by then obvious fact that "no one would contend that the legislature could

[9]261 U.S. at 557–58 (quotation marks indicating quotations from prior cases omitted).
[10]Ibid., at 546.

take A's property and give it to B," he added a new example, one not destined for enduring fame but indicative of the state of the law at the time: "or enact a law that no one under six feet in height should be allowed to sell groceries."[11] Outlawing short grocers, in Hughes's opinion, was just as obviously bad as taking from A and giving to B. Although the prohibition operated in favor of tall people, Hughes did not think of it as a simple transfer from one group to another; otherwise, he would have had no reason to add it to the A-to-B example.[12] The problem, in other words, had been generalized into one of arbitrary government action, taking away something of value with no corresponding public gain. Littleton and Coke would have pronounced it "against common right and reason."

Fifty years before Hughes spoke, the U.S. Supreme Court in *Allgeyer v. Louisiana* (1897)[13] had for the first time held that it was a violation of due process to deprive a person of

[11]Charles Evans Hughes, *The Supreme Court of the United States* (New York: Columbia University Press, 1928), 195–96. Hughes had been an associate justice of the U.S. Supreme Court from 1910 to 1916; he returned to the Court as chief justice in 1930. Of notably short stature, Hughes may have intended a visual joke by his example of a law confining the grocery business to tall men.

[12]It was long ago pointed out that "nearly every law transfers something from A to B." Robert Luce, *Legislative Problems: Development, Status, and Trend of the Treatment and Exercise of Lawmaking Powers* (Boston: Houghton Mifflin, 1935), 60. It is not my purpose in this book, nor would it be within my competence, to trace the economic consequences of all the statutes invalidated for violation of the due process clause.

[13]165 U.S. 578 (1897).

the right to make contracts, a taking from A unaccompanied by any obvious giving to B. Invalidated was a state law that forbade obtaining marine insurance on in-state property from an insurance company that was not registered to do business within the state. At issue was a contract of insurance entered into by Allgeyer in New York with an out-of-state insurance company concerning a shipment of cotton from New Orleans to foreign ports. If Louisiana law could constitutionally prohibit that, then it could literally take something from A: the opportunity to make an enforceable agreement that, though relating to objects physically within the state, did not affect state interests. It was (and remained) unclear whether what was taken was A's property or contract: "In the privilege of pursuing an ordinary calling or trade and of acquiring, holding and selling property," the Court said, "must be embraced the right to make all proper contracts in relation thereto."[14]

Insurance is an important industry, key to economic development, but contracts of insurance form only a tiny fraction of all contracts. In terms of economic and social

[14]Ibid., at 591. Scholars often trace the origin of substantive due process in the U.S. Supreme Court to Justice Stephen J. Field's dissenting opinion in the *Slaughter House Cases,* in which he listed a series of individual liberties supposedly immune from government interference, among them "the right to pursue a lawful employment in a lawful manner, without other restraint than such as equally affects all persons" (83 U.S. [16 Wall.] 36, 83, 97 [1873] [Field, J., dissenting]). See Roscoe Pound, "Liberty of Contract," *Yale Law Journal* 18 (1909): 454.

importance, they pale in comparison with contracts of employment, the means for the mobilization of labor, and it was with respect to employment contracts that due process was to exhibit its greatest and most controversial development. The most famous (or infamous) substantive due process case ever decided by the U.S. Supreme Court was *Lochner v. New York*[15] in 1905. Striking down a New York statute limiting the hours of labor for bakers to sixty hours a week or ten hours a day, *Lochner* gave its name to the entire era in the history of due process from the 1890s to the 1930s, during which courts strictly scrutinized regulatory legislation, particularly labor legislation, enacted pursuant to the state's general power to protect public health, safety, or welfare—known to lawyers as the "police power."[16] According to the Court, the question to be answered in *Lochner* was, "Is this a fair, reasonable and appropriate exercise of the police power of the State, or is it an unreasonable, unnecessary and arbitrary interference with the right of the

[15]198 U.S. 45 (1905). The literature on *Lochner* is vast. The most comprehensive account is Paul Kens, *Judicial Power and Reform Politics: The Anatomy of* Lochner v. New York (Lawrence: University Press of Kansas, 1990). But see the review by James W. Ely Jr., "Economic Due Process Revisited," *Vanderbilt Law Review* 44 (1991): 213–20. See also Matthew S. Bewig, "Lochner v. The Journeymen Bakers of New York: The Journeymen Bakers, Their Hours of Labor, and the Constitution," *American Journal of Legal History* 38 (1994): 413–51.

[16]Although the court invalidated the hours provision of the Bakeshop Act, it upheld various hygienic and structural standards for bakeries (198 U.S., at 61–62).

individual to his personal liberty or to enter into those contracts in relation to labor which may seem to him appropriate or necessary for the support of himself and his family?"[17]
In other words, should the state substitute its decision for
that of an (adult) male worker? Put in those terms, it is
hardly surprising that the Court found the Bakeshop Act
not reasonably related to any of the social ends for which
government power might validly be exercised and therefore
a violation of the due process clause.[18]

Again, it was not exactly clear what was taken by the
statute at issue in *Lochner,* or from whom. Although Adam
Smith had convinced some American judges that labor was
property,[19] the usage had not generally caught on. Yet it was
obvious to the judges that *something* had been taken: if not
property in labor, then "personal liberty," or the right to con-

[17]198 U.S., at 56.

[18]The dissenters in *Lochner,* including Justice Oliver Wendell Holmes,
who wrote a vigorous and oft-quoted dissent, put the question differ-
ently: whether the court should defer to the legislative judgment.

[19]Compare Adam Smith, *An Inquiry into the Nature and Causes of the
Wealth of Nations* (1776; reprint, New York: Modern Library, 1937), 121
("the property which every man has in his own labour, as it is the original foundation of all other property, so it is the most sacred and invio-
lable") with *Butchers' Union Co. v. Crescent City Co.,* 111 U.S. 746, 765 (1884)
("and if a man's right to his calling is property, as many maintain, then
those who had already adopted the prohibited pursuits in New Orleans,
were deprived, by the law in question, of their property, as well as their
liberty, without due process of law"), and at 757 (Field, J., concurring)
(quoting *The Wealth of Nations*).

tract with respect to labor, from the employer who bought labor as well as from the employee who sold it. By the end of the nineteenth century, contract (the legal means for the organization of economic life) had become almost as important as property (the legal right to the enjoyment of present or past economic gains). In England, the birthplace of the Industrial Revolution, the respected jurist Sir George Jessel had announced in 1875, "If there is one thing more than another which public policy requires, it is that men of full age and competent understanding shall have the utmost liberty of contracting." "Freedom of contract" is, he added, "paramount public policy."[20] But English judges were working without a constitutional text; in the nineteenth century, as a hundred years earlier during the age of Blackstone, they had no power to declare acts of Parliament void.

In America, by contrast, "paramount public policy" was to be found in the constitutions, state and federal. Although, unlike their English brethren, American judges had the undoubted power of judicial review, they were supposed to confine its exercise to textual violations. It must have seemed somewhat puzzling to them at the time that the due process clause singled out only life, liberty, and property for special protection. Where was contract? Following Jessel's

[20]*Printing & Numerical Registering Co. v. Sampson*, L.R. 19 Eq. 462, 465 (1875). Fifty years later Benjamin Cardozo, in *Lochner*-era America, recalled, perhaps sardonically, Jessel's "often quoted judgment." See Benjamin N. Cardozo, *The Nature of the Judicial Process* (New Haven: Yale University Press, 1921), 67.

clue, they were able to find it included in liberty. The creativity of this solution should be recognized. In his catalog of the "absolute rights of Englishmen," written in 1765 on the eve of the American Revolution, Blackstone had defined liberty in the most obvious terms as "the power of locomotion, of changing situation, or removing one's person to whatsoever place one's own inclination may direct; without imprisonment or restraint, unless by due course of law," and he had found its safeguard in the great writ of habeas corpus.[21] Contract, notable only by its absence from Blackstone's magisterial survey of English law, found no place in his catalog of rights. But by an expansive understanding of liberty, the American judiciary a century later could vastly extend the reach of the due process clause. "Liberty of contracting" or simply "freedom of contract," as the Court expressly held in the District of Columbia minimum wage case, gained for a time a constitutional footing.[22]

In *Lochner* there was an obvious taking but no obvious giving, so the A-to-B paradigm was not directly relevant, although the judges seemed to have suspected something: "It is impossible to shut our eyes to the fact," they said, "that

[21]William Blackstone, *Commentaries on the Laws of England* (Oxford, 1765), 1: 130–34.

[22]"Freedom of contract" should more properly be called "freedom *to* contract," but the former phrase was the one regularly used at the time. I have retained it here not only because of its contemporaneous usage but also because it nicely expresses the extent to which contract had become personified, as if "contract" itself could have rights.

many of the laws of this character, while passed under what is claimed to be the police power for the purpose of protecting the public health or welfare, are, in reality, passed from other motives."[23] What other motives they thought might be lurking can only be guessed at: a desire to raise wages by restricting hours (a transfer from employer to employee)? A desire to increase overall employment by limiting individual hours of labor (a transfer from some workers to others)? Or a desire to disadvantage certain groups who needed to work longer hours to compete (a transfer from those put out of work to those at work)? So strong is the association between substantive due process and taking from A and giving to B that twentieth-century legal commentators continue to describe *Lochner* in A-to-B terms, without specifying the identity of the persons behind the labels.[24] From the judges' point of view, the giving part of the equation seemed less important; taking had become the problem.

Freedom of contract as applied to contracts of employment was obviously consequential. Labor is an essential ingredient in economic production. But the importance of the newfound freedom was even greater than first appears. The employment contract once meant the hiring contract. Would a worker agree to work? If so, the relationship tradi-

[23]198 U.S., at 64.

[24]Cass Sunstein, "Naked Preferences and the Constitution," *Columbia Law Review* 84 (1984): 1689, 1717; Laurence H. Tribe, *American Constitutional Law* (Mineola, N.Y.: Foundation Press, 1978), 439.

tionally known as "master and servant" was created. At one time, the law filled in most of the details of service.[25] But by the time *Lochner* was decided, the employment contract had come to mean an agreement that governed every aspect of the working relationship.[26] When, years earlier, Chancellor Kent in his influential *Commentaries on American Law* had stated that "this relation of master and servant rests altogether on contract,"[27] he may have meant little more than that no one is a servant who has not agreed to be one, but the statement could also be read to mean that all the terms of the master-servant relationship were governed by the agreement. It was this expansive understanding of contract that informed the decision in *Lochner.* The individual contract of employment, not the statute book, seemed to be the proper place to set the hours of labor.

As American workers came to realize the obstacles to legislative remedies for their problems, not only the complicated enactment process and the jurisdictional patchwork of state and federal governments but also the time-consuming and

[25]See John V. Orth, *Combination and Conspiracy: A Legal History of Trade Unionism, 1721–1906* (Oxford: Clarendon Press, 1991), 3–21.

[26]See John V. Orth, "Contract and the Common Law," in *The State and Freedom of Contract,* ed. Harry N. Scheiber (Stanford, Calif.: Stanford University Press, 1998), 44–65.

[27]James Kent, *Commentaries on American Law,* ed. O.W. Holmes, 12th ed. (Boston, 1873), 2: 258. Kent himself immediately made it plain that "there are many important legal consequences which flow from this relation of master and servant," that is, from the relationship, not from the contract (259).

unpredictable course of judicial review, they turned their attention more to the gains that could be attained by collective action through labor unions.[28] In many industries, especially where skilled labor was involved, unions made significant progress. Employers in some industries countered by invoking the newly potent power of contract, requiring their workers to agree as a condition of employment that they would not join a labor organization, an agreement that acquired the colorful name "yellow dog contract."[29] Workers struck back, using their political power to secure legislation, federal as well as state, prohibiting such contracts, but federal courts invalidated both types of statutes as infringements of freedom of contract and therefore violations of the due process clause.[30] The uncertainty about whether what was taken was liberty or property continued, the Court holding in one case that "the right to make contracts for the acquisition of property" is "included in the right of personal liberty and the right of private property—partaking of the nature of each."[31]

[28]The same thing had happened earlier in England. See Orth, *Combination and Conspiracy*, 68–98.

[29]The name seems to come from the usage of "yellow dog," a cur or mongrel, to mean anything contemptible (*Oxford Companion to the Supreme Court of the United States*, ed. Kermit L. Hall [New York: Oxford University Press, 1992], 948). In England the comparable agreement was called simply "the document." See Orth, *Combination and Conspiracy*, 129.

[30]*Adair v. United States*, 208 U.S. 161 (1908) (holding federal statute a violation of the Fifth Amendment due process clause); *Coppage v. Kansas*, 236 U.S. 1 (1915) (holding state statute a violation of the Fourteenth Amendment due process clause).

[31]236 U.S., at 14.

As the emphasis shifted to taking from A, giving to B became an increasingly vestigial part of the A-to-B paradigm.
Having limbered up, as it were, on the longer version, the
judges were now ready for the short form. Although the A-
to-B paradigm had once seemed only another example of
procedural irregularity, it had in time acquired another
meaning, substantive rather than procedural. In some cases
property simply could not be taken, no matter by whom, no
matter for what. As with property, so with contract. Taking
away the right to contract—as, for example, with respect to
wages, hours, or whether to join a union—was arguably a
violation, if not exactly of due process then at least of the example that had so long been used to illustrate its abuse. But
before examining the final due process paradigm and its application to noneconomic or social issues, we must first take
note of a major deflection in American constitutional history. By the late 1930s substantive economic due process and
other legal doctrines restricting economic regulation had
become a political issue of the greatest magnitude.

On March 9, 1937, President Franklin Roosevelt addressed
the nation on radio, one of his periodic "fireside chats." "My
Friends," he began, and launched a remarkable assault on the
Supreme Court of the United States: "We have . . . reached
the point as a Nation where we must take action to save the
Constitution from the Court and the Court from itself. We
must find a way to take an appeal from the Supreme Court
to the Constitution itself. We want a Supreme Court which
will do justice under the Constitution—not over it. In our

courts we want a government of laws and not of men."[32] Within days the president's supporters in Congress introduced the Court Reform bill, better known to history as the "court-packing plan," designed to secure a majority of justices to uphold the government's economic program.[33] Authorizing the president to appoint one new justice for every sitting justice over the age of seventy, the bill provided for a maximum complement of as many as fifteen judges.[34]

The proximate cause of the president's action was frustration over the judicial veto of so many items of his economic program, a dozen in the years from 1934 to 1936. But in a larger sense, the confrontation between the political and judicial branches had been building for many years. Beginning in the 1890s, the courts—state as well as federal—had embarked on an increasingly active role in screening social legislation.[35] As Oliver Wendell Holmes pungently put it in 1897, while still a justice of the Massachusetts Supreme Judicial Court, "People who no longer hope to control the legislatures . . . look to the courts as expounders of the Constitutions, and . . . in some courts new principles have been discovered outside

[32]*Public Papers and Addresses of Franklin D. Roosevelt, 1937*, ed. Samuel I. Rosenman (New York: Random House, 1941), 122.

[33]See William E. Leuchtenburg, *The Supreme Court Reborn: The Constitutional Revolution in the Age of Roosevelt* (New York: Oxford University Press, 1995), 82, 132; John V. Orth, "How Many Judges Does It Take to Make a Supreme Court?" *Constitutional Commentary*, forthcoming.

[34]S. Rept. no. 711, 75th Cong., 1st Sess., 31 (1937).

[35]See William E. Leuchtenburg, *The Perils of Prosperity, 1914–1932* (Chicago: University of Chicago Press, 1958), 99–100.

the bodies of those instruments, which may be generalized into acceptance of economic doctrines which prevailed about fifty years ago."[36] Substantive due process was one of the "new principles" Holmes had in mind.[37]

Roosevelt's Court Reform bill was never adopted, foundering on a public consensus that it would have too obviously politicized the judicial branch. But a majority of the sitting justices rather suddenly coalesced in support of the president's program, abandoning economic substantive due process and discovering rather belatedly, as then Chief Justice Charles Evans Hughes put it, that "the Constitution does not speak of freedom of contract"[38]—the so-called "switch in time that saved nine."[39] As one knowledgeable observer com-

[36] Oliver Wendell Holmes, "The Path of the Law," *Harvard Law Review* 10 (1897): 457, 467–68.

[37] Holmes repeated his criticism in his celebrated dissent in *Lochner*, which began, "This case is decided upon an economic theory which a large part of the country does not entertain" (198 U.S., at 75 [Holmes, J., dissenting]).

[38] *West Coast Hotel Co. v. Parrish*, 300 U.S. 379, 391 (1937) (upholding minimum wage law and overruling *Adkins*).

[39] The provenance of this phrase is discussed in Michael Ariens, "A Thrice-Told Tale, or Felix the Cat," *Harvard Law Review* 107 (1994): 620, 623 n. 11. Whether the "switch" was in response to the court-packing plan has been the subject of debate. See Richard D. Friedman, "A Reaffirmation: The Authenticity of the Roberts Memorandum, or Felix the Non-Forger," *University of Pennsylvania Law Review* 142 (1994): 1985–95. See also Barry Cushman, *Rethinking the New Deal Court: The Structure of a Constitutional Revolution* (New York: Oxford University Press, 1998), reviewed by William Lasser, "Justice Roberts and the Constitutional Revolution of 1937—Was There a 'Switch in Time'?" *Texas Law Review* 78 (2000): 1347–76.

mented, "Each side of the controversy comforted itself with a claim of victory. The President's enemies defeated the court reform bill—the President achieved court reform."[40]

Barely a year after the president's fireside chat the Supreme Court spelled out its new approach. *United States v. Carolene Products Co.*[41] concerned the constitutionality of congressional legislation that prohibited the interstate shipment of "filled milk," that is, skim milk mixed with any fat or oil other than milk fat. A few years earlier the legislation would have had to run the gauntlet of judicial scrutiny. During the *Lochner* era the question would have been whether the statute appeared to the judges to be "fair, reasonable and appropriate" or an "unreasonable, unnecessary and arbitrary interference" with freedom of contract, but in *Carolene Products* the Court announced a new standard. Henceforth it would defer to the legislature on the question of reasonableness—"the existence of facts supporting the legislative judgment is to be presumed"[42]—thereby shifting the burden of proof from those supporting the legislation to those opposing it. The new presumption of constitutionality would apply to all "regulatory legislation affecting ordinary commercial transactions."[43]

Having gone out of the business of second-guessing the

[40]Robert Jackson, successively solicitor general, attorney general, and U.S. Supreme Court justice, quoted in Bernard Schwartz, *The Law in America* (New York: McGraw Hill, 1974), 198.

[41]304 U.S. 144 (1938).

[42]Ibid., at 152.

[43]Ibid.

legislature's regulatory decisions, what was left of the Supreme Court's historic mission? Statutory construction, oversight of state courts, reconciliation of conflicting decisions of the federal courts of appeals—none of the ordinary and necessary work of a court of last resort compared with the high constitutional business of rulings on constitutionality. Now that ordinary regulatory legislation enjoyed a presumption in its favor, a large part of the Supreme Court's former workload—and some of the most noteworthy—was gone. In a now famous footnote appended to the sentence announcing the new policy, the Court made clear that its surrender was accompanied by a challenge and hinted at a new role for itself. Although laws "affecting ordinary commercial transactions" would be presumed reasonable and therefore constitutional, laws affecting other constitutional rights would not be treated so generously.

The effect was to reduce the judicial protection afforded property (and contract), at least when involved in commercial transactions, and to redirect judicial scrutiny to other constitutional rights. Thus was born the doctrine of "preferred freedoms"[44]—critics still denounce it as a "double standard"[45]—the notion that some rights are entitled to

[44]For a brief overview, see James Willard Hurst, *Dealing with Statutes* (New York: Columbia University Press, 1982), 99–106.

[45]Michael J. Phillips, *The Lochner Court, Myth and Reality: Substantive Due Process from the 1890s to the 1930s* (Westport, Conn.: Praeger, 2001), 24, 185–92; Frank R. Strong, *Substantive Due Process of Law: A Dichotomy of Sense and Nonsense* (Durham, N.C.: Carolina Academic Press, 1986), 160.

more judicial protection than others, despite the textual equivalence in the due process clauses of "life, liberty, and property." The *Carolene Products* footnote singled out for protection the political processes of representative democracy and the rights of certain minorities who might be unable to protect themselves through the political process.[46] From this little seed much of the constitutional history of the last half of the twentieth century grew, particularly the judicial branch of the civil rights movement. In the meantime, economic substantive due process was dead.

[46]The famous footnote appears as follows, omitting only case citations:

There may be narrower scope for operation of the presumption of constitutionality when legislation appears on its face to be within a specific prohibition of the Constitution, such as those of the first ten amendments, which are deemed equally specific when held to be embraced within the Fourteenth. . . .

It is unnecessary to consider now whether legislation which restricts those political processes which can ordinarily be expected to bring about repeal of undesirable legislation, is to be subjected to more exacting judicial scrutiny under the general prohibitions of the Fourteenth Amendment than are most other types of legislation. . . .

Nor need we enquire whether similar considerations enter into the review of statutes directed at particular religious . . . or national . . . or racial minorities: whether prejudice against discrete and insular minorities may be a special condition, which tends seriously to curtail the operation of those political processes ordinarily to be relied upon to protect minorities, and which may call for a correspondingly more searching judicial inquiry.

304 U.S., at 152 n. 4. See also Peter Linzer, "The *Carolene Products* Footnote and the Preferred Position of Individual Rights: Louis Lusky and John Hart Ely vs. Harlan Fiske Stone," *Constitutional Commentary* 12 (1995): 277–303.

5

Case III. Taking from A:
Noneconomic Substantive Due Process

Were due process merely a procedural safeguard it would fail to
reach those situations where the deprivation of life, liberty or
property was accomplished by legislation which by operating in
the future could, given even the fairest possible procedure ... ,
nevertheless destroy the enjoyment of all three. . . . Thus the
guaranties of due process, though having their roots in Magna
Carta's *"per legem terrae"* and considered as procedural safeguards
"against executive usurpation and tyranny," have in this country
"become bulwarks also against arbitrary legislation."

JOHN MARSHALL HARLAN, J. (1961)

The taking-from-A-and-giving-to-B paradigm had come
to be tied to the use of substantive due process in cases
concerning economic regulation, so its eclipse as a reference
point in federal constitutional law was inevitable once the
U.S. Supreme Court announced in the *Carolene Products* case

a general presumption in favor of the constitutionality of "regulatory legislation affecting ordinary commercial transactions." Although Charles Evans Hughes had told his audience at Columbia in 1927 that it was equally unimaginable that a legislature could be permitted to take A's property and give it to B *or* outlaw the sale of groceries by anyone under six feet tall, his first example had now to be discarded. Such simple (or simplistic) paradigms had in any event become embarrassments, as legal discourse, increasingly influenced by academic legal education, displayed new sophistication. But the concept of substantive due process that the A-to-B paradigm had helped to midwife did not pass away.

Hughes's second example, a statute outlawing short grocers, provides a clue to later developments. Although equally rooted in commercial life, it discards the transactional element of the A-to-B paradigm and focuses instead on the taking aspect: taking away from short people the opportunity to participate in the grocery trade. On one level, it illustrates government interference with the operations of the free market, advantaging favored market participants (tall grocers) to the disadvantage of others (short grocers)— and of the consuming public as well. But on another level, it illustrates the loss of individual liberty, commercial in this case but generalizable to include the unjustified taking away of any liberty. Taking and giving is redistributional, reassigning the indicia of wealth or power; taking is simple subtraction. Wrenched from its economic context and transformed into a prohibition of arbitrary legislation in noneconomic or social matters, the taking paradigm remained to see active duty later in a new class of cases concerning claimed violations of individual privacy.

Taking from A and giving to B had directed jurists' attention to successive violations of due process: first to the usurpation by the legislature of the judiciary's role in determining title to real property (separation of powers), then to interference with contract and the individual economic ordering it permitted (freedom of contract), and finally to restraints on freedom in general. This new emphasis combined with the attention to civil rights announced in the now famous footnote in the *Carolene Products* case to give additional substance to due process, as liberty came to be defined in terms other than economic. Supreme Court Justice David Souter has observed that *Allgeyer v. Louisiana*, the 1897 case that first proclaimed freedom of contract, "offered a substantive interpretation of 'liberty,' that in the aftermath of the so-called *Lochner* Era has been scaled back in some respects, but expanded in others, and never repudiated in principle."[1] The scaling back came in the area of economic substantive due process, while the expansion occurred in cases of noneconomic rights, especially in cases involving human reproduction. But before the development of substantive due process could resume, the ghosts of the 1930s and economic substantive due process had first to be exorcised.

---

[1] *Washington v. Glucksberg,* 521 U.S. 702, 760 (1997) (Souter, J., concurring).

For thirty years after *Carolene Products,* substantive due process seemed to be dead. In a 1963 case upholding a state law that limited the business of debt collecting to lawyers, the justices of the Supreme Court seemed to bury it in no uncertain terms: "We emphatically refuse to go back to the time when courts used the Due Process Clause 'to strike down state laws, regulatory of business and industrial conditions, because they may be unwise, improvident, or out of harmony with a particular school of thought.'"[2] The justices pointedly declined even to ask what might be called the "*Lochner* question": whether the statute was a "fair, reasonable, and appropriate" interference with freedom of contract in the pursuit of an ordinary trade or calling.[3] Instead, they simply deferred to the legislative judgment.

Nor was the demise of substantive due process apparently limited to its economic form alone. Even in cases not involving freedom of contract and not entitled to the presumption in favor of ordinary regulatory legislation, the due process clause seemed largely irrelevant. In 1965 in *Griswold v. Con-*

---

[2] *Ferguson v. Skrupa,* 372 U.S. 726, 731 (1963) (quoting *Williamson v. Lee Optical, Inc.,* 348 U.S. 483, 488 [1955]). State courts were not necessarily so deferential. See Joshua A. Newberg, "In Defense of *Aston Park:* The Case for State Substantive Due Process Review of Health Care Regulation," *North Carolina Law Review* 68 (1990): 253, 263–68.

[3] This question actually conflates *Lochner's* emphasis on a judicial finding of reasonableness and *Allgeyer's* emphasis on freedom of contract with respect to one's occupation.

necticut,[4] the Supreme Court invalidated a state statute prohibiting artificial birth control because it invaded "zones of privacy" recognized by various amendments in the Bill of Rights and applied to the states by the Fourteenth Amendment: the First Amendment's right of association, the Third Amendment's prohibition against the peacetime quartering of soldiers in private homes without consent, the Fourth Amendment's protection against unreasonable searches and seizures, the Fifth Amendment's privilege against self-incrimination, and the Ninth Amendment's reservation to the people of unenumerated rights. Although the due process clause of the Fourteenth Amendment was involved in *Griswold,* its role was simply to serve as the vehicle through which specific parts of the Bill of Rights, otherwise applicable only to the federal government, were applied to the states.[5] Notable by its absence was the Fifth Amendment's due process clause.

[4]381 U.S. 479 (1965). The statute had been before the court previously in *Poe v. Ullman,* 367 U.S. 497 (1961), where the court held that the controversy was not ripe for resolution because the plaintiff had not actually been prosecuted. Justice John Marshall Harlan II dissented, finding the issue justiciable and making a powerful statement in favor of substantive due process, from which the epigraph of this chapter is taken; see *Poe,* at 541 (Harlan, J., dissenting) (quoting *Hurtado v. California,* 110 U.S. 516, 532 [1884]). The Court subsequently accepted Harlan's reasoning in *Planned Parenthood of Southeastern Pennsylvania v. Casey,* 505 U.S. 833, 848–49 (1992).

[5]The exact function of the Ninth Amendment in the Court's decision in *Griswold* was unclear; since it reserves unenumerated rights to the people, it could hardly be "applied to the states" through the Fourteenth Amendment. Its use seems to have been primarily to enrich the concept of "liberty" protected by the Fourteenth Amendment.

Whatever the Court said, *Griswold* in fact opened a new era of substantive due process, one concerned with noneconomic rights, as was shortly made plain in *Roe v. Wade*,[6] the 1973 abortion decision. A too-restrictive abortion law was held to violate a woman's right to privacy, now simply described as an aspect of liberty. To pass constitutional muster the law had to advance a legitimate government interest in the least intrusive manner; in other words, it had to be "fair, reasonable, and appropriate"—the *Lochner* formula minus the economic context. "A state criminal abortion statute of the current Texas type, that excepts from criminality only a *life-saving* procedure on behalf of the mother, without regard to pregnancy stage and without recognition of the other interests involved," the Court held, "is violative of the Due Process Clause of the Fourteenth Amendment."[7] The due process clause is now itself the source of the restriction, not merely the conduit through which parts of the Bill of Rights are applied to the states. Concurring in *Roe*, Justice Potter Stewart revealed the new understanding of the earlier birth control case: "The *Griswold* decision can be rationally understood only as a holding that the Connecticut statute substantively invaded the 'liberty' that is protected by the Due Process Clause of the Fourteenth

---

[6] 410 U.S. 113 (1973).

[7] Ibid., at 164 ("life-saving" is in italics in the original to emphasize that the exception was too restrictive).

Amendment,"[8] thus beginning the recharacterization of *Griswold* as a substantive due process case that has gained acceptance by commentators and justices alike.[9]

Both the birth control and the abortion cases involved an invasion of privacy, what might once have been called a "taking" of liberty in violation of the due process clause. In the heyday of economic substantive due process, comparable invasions of privacy had been addressed, albeit with some difficulty, as impermissible commercial regulation. When a state, spurred by war-induced xenophobia in 1919, outlawed the teaching of foreign languages in primary schools, the U.S. Supreme Court found it a violation of the teacher's "right to teach" and the parents' right to contract with teachers for the instruction of their children.[10] And when nativist passion in the 1920s led another state to outlaw private schools, including private religious schools, the Court found it an unwarranted interference with business and property, although the schools' religious proprietors were obviously responding to a call higher than the profit

[8]Ibid., at 168 (Stewart, J., concurring). As Stewart observed, three other justices at the time *Griswold* was decided had also thought it concerned substantive due process; see 381 U.S., at 499 (Harlan, J., concurring in judgment); at 502 (White, J., concurring in judgment); and at 507 (Black, J., dissenting).

[9]See, e.g., *Planned Parenthood of Southeastern Pennsylvania v. Casey*, 505 U.S. 833, 846–53 (1992), and *County of Sacramento v. Lewis*, 523 U.S. 833, 846 (1998). See also Frank R. Strong, *Substantive Due Process of Law: A Dichotomy of Sense and Nonsense* (Durham, N.C.: Carolina Academic Press, 1986), 109–13.

[10]*Meyer v. Nebraska*, 262 U.S. 390, 400 (1923).

motive.[11] At the time of decision the cases could be analogized to interferences with the free market; today they are generally understood as involving an aspect of liberty other than freedom of contract, perhaps a First Amendment right of free speech or association, or a family's right to privacy.[12] Liberty, which Blackstone had defined as unrestrained locomotion, and which nineteenth-century jurists had redefined to include freedom of contract, had now become "the right to be let alone."[13]

The old emphasis on economic rights and the consequent implication of property and contract had all but disappeared in the new era; it lingered only in the vestigial reference to the professional relationship between doctor and patient in the field of human reproduction, and even there the emphasis was not on the economics of the medical services industry. But the former solicitude for economic rights had played a role in getting the Court to accept its new mission as defender of personal autonomy. The protection of property in all its forms led insensibly to a protection of contract, which might, after all, be described as "property in

---

[11]*Pierce v. Society of Sisters,* 268 U.S. 510 (1925).

[12]See, e.g., *Griswold,* 381 U.S., at 482 (describing *Meyer* and *Pierce* as standing for the proposition that "the State may not . . . contract the spectrum of available knowledge").

[13]For the phrase, "the right to be let alone," see *Olmstead v. United States,* 277 U.S. 438, 478 (1928) (Brandeis, J., dissenting); Samuel D. Warren and Louis D. Brandeis, "The Right to Privacy," *Harvard Law Review* 4 (1890): 193.

motion."[14] (Liberty protected the dynamic element; hence, liberty or freedom of contract.) The protection of contract had in turn directed attention to the primacy of the individual will, so interference with intention or expectation came in time to seem as egregious as interference with property and, unless justified by a compelling government interest, just as impermissible. Rights had come to be thought of as expectations people had, as much as (or more than) things they were entitled to.[15]

Lacking the economic context, agreement on what is acceptable has been hard to find. Charles Evans Hughes's extreme example of a statute outlawing short grocers might well command the same broad condemnation today that it did in 1927. If so, the reason would be the pervasive acceptance of some idea of economic rationality as well as a widespread social commitment to equality. There is simply no reasonable connection between the business of selling groceries and the grocer's height. The adoption of such a statute would inevitably engender the same dark thoughts that bothered the judges in *Lochner*: there must be a hidden motive, probably a desire to favor a cabal of wealthy, well-

[14]See John V. Orth, "Contract and the Common Law," in *The State and Freedom of Contract,* ed. Harry N. Scheiber (Stanford, Calif.: Stanford University Press, 1998), 44, 49.

[15]Rights in property have been progressively relabeled, under the influence of contract-thinking, "expectations," specifically "investment-backed expectations." See *Penn Central Transportation Co. v. City of New York,* 438 U.S. 104, 123–28 (1978).

connected—and tall—individuals. Today the problem might more naturally be seen as discrimination against short persons and, if expressed in a state statute, correspondingly addressed under the equal protection clause of the Fourteenth Amendment: "No state shall ... deny to any person within its jurisdiction the equal protection of the laws." Since the equal protection clause applies only to the states, were a federal statute involved, recourse would have to be made to the all-purpose due process clause of the Fifth Amendment.[16]

Attention is rightly paid to substantive due process as a restraint on legislative power; many applications of the doctrine, new and old, have been controversial, and its historical development has carried due process the farthest from its roots. But frequent appeal to the requirements of due process in challenges to legislation, state and federal, should not obscure the fact that executive action is still subject to the restraints of due process. Just as the procedural aspect of due process preceded the substantive, so the limitation on the executive was prior to that on the legislature; and just as the procedural safeguards of due process became in addition substantive prohibitions against arbitrary legislation, so the procedural safeguards against executive tyranny have become substantive restraints against arbitrary executive action.

---

[16]See *Bolling v. Sharpe,* 347 U.S. 497, 499 (1954) ("the concepts of equal protection and due process, both stemming from our American ideal of fairness, are not mutually exclusive"; "discrimination may be so unjustifiable as to be violative of due process").

Although nearly eight hundred years have passed since English barons, sword in hand, forced King John to swear not "to go or send against any free man except *per legem terrae* [by the law of the land]," claims that executive misconduct violates due process continue to trouble the courts today. Clearly the sovereign and its officers—the American executive no less than the medieval English monarch—must observe proper procedures, including the need for impartiality (not making a man a judge in his own case).[17] But the substance of executive action too must conform to the judicial standard of due process; otherwise, executive tyranny could pass muster if all the proper forms were observed. Even if procedural due process is satisfied, executive action may be so disproportionate to proper governmental ends that due process in another sense may be violated. Here again arbitrariness is the test, although only the most egregious official action depriving a person of life, liberty, or property has been found arbitrary: action that "shocks the conscience" and violates the "decencies of civilized conduct."[18] Here, too, concerning specific applications, it has proved just as difficult to find judicial (or societal) consensus on the arbitrariness that renders executive

[17]See *Goldberg v. Kelly*, 397 U.S. 254 (1970), discussed in chapter 6.

[18]*County of Sacramento v. Lewis*, 523 U.S. 833, 846 (1998) (quoting *Rochin v. California*, 342 U.S. 165, 172 [1952]). For a case struggling with the distinction between legislative and executive action and the different due process standards applied to each, see *Hawkins v. Freeman*, 195 F.3d 732 (4th Cir. 1999).

action violative of due process: as Justice Iredell reminded Justice Chase so long ago, on such matters "the ablest and purest minds have differed."

6

Conclusion. Due Process of Law: Procedure and Substance

Out of ould fields must spring and grow the new Corne.
SIR EDWARD COKE (1628)

In a system based on precedent nothing is ever truly lost. The history of the law of due process marked by the succession of paradigm cases has been accretive: new paradigms have added to the content of the law.[1] When two hundred years ago the A-to-B paradigm pulled alongside "making a man a judge in his own case," it first complemented the procedural content of due process, then added a growing substantive element. In the 1930s the exuberant growth of substantive due process was pruned, as "regula-

---

[1]See John V. Orth, "The Mystery of the Rule in Shelley's Case," in *Green Bag*, 2d ser. (forthcoming), arguing that the common law is better at adding than subtracting.

tory legislation affecting ordinary commercial transactions"
was presumed to satisfy the due process clause without independent judicial scrutiny. After a brief period of disorien-
tation, the development of substantive due process resumed,
as it became apparent that the substance of due process was
not solely economic. Experience with the taking-from-A-
and-giving-to-B paradigm had revealed that taking was
more important than giving, even when economic rights
were involved. Outside the economic context, the transfer
of value implicit in taking and giving made little sense. Taking from A was particularly appropriate to describe interference with noneconomic or social interests.

Case I: Making a Man a Judge in His Own Case

Due process still forbids, and always will, unfair procedures.
Although the paradigm of making a man a judge in his own
case is rarely heard of these days, the underlying concern remains vital. Corrupt, partial, or fearful decision makers cannot dispense justice and are not even properly called judges.
Other abuses rival the unjust judge as a violation of due
process: absence of a hearing, inadequate time to prepare,
denial of legal representation, and more—enough to fill a
chamber of procedural horrors.[2]

[2]For a list of twenty-two cases decided between 1897 and 1937 in which
the U.S. Supreme Court struck down government action because it was

The operational meaning of fairness was undergoing development by the common law even as the American constitutions, state and federal, adopted as a standard "the law of the land" or "due process of law," phrases that encoded a whole tradition of procedural propriety. Sir Edward Coke gave due process content when he insisted in *Dr. Bonham's Case* (1610) on the imperative need for an impartial judge. Although Sir William Blackstone, on behalf of the English legal community in the eighteenth century, receded from Coke's position and announced a reluctant recognition of parliamentary supremacy, the American judiciary took up where Coke had left off and, finding in the constitutions a source of "higher law," embraced judicial review. In America, at least, courts had the power to prevent a legislature from making a man a judge in his own case.[3] Even today, after so many centuries, the demands of proper procedure are still being elaborated.[4]

---

not accompanied by adequate notice, a fair trial or hearing, or a closely related procedural requirement, see Michael J. Phillips, *The Lochner Court, Myth and Reality: Substantive Due Process from the 1890s to the 1930s* (Westport, Conn.: Praeger, 2001), 35 and 65 n. 30.

[3] *Tumey v. Ohio*, 273 U.S. 510 (1928). *Tumey* is one of the cases on the list cited in the preceding note. For a later case, see *Connally v. Georgia*, 429 U.S. 245 (1977) (holding unconstitutional a state statute providing that justices of the peace are paid a fee for issuing a search warrant but not for denying one).

[4] See, e.g., *BMW of North America v. Gore*, 517 U.S. 559 (1996) (holding invalid a large punitive damages award because of inadequate notice to the defendant of the magnitude of the potential sanction). Illustrating the

Procedural due process, far from being a mere requirement of technical fastidiousness, retains the potential to unsettle the powerful. In 1970 in *Goldberg v. Kelly*[5] the U.S. Supreme Court was asked to rule on what a state had to do before it could cut off welfare benefits to the indigent. Due process requires a hearing, the Court said, and spelled out exactly what that means: (1) adequate notice, (2) an opportunity to be heard, (3) the right to present evidence, (4) confrontation of opposing witnesses, (5) the right to cross-examine those witnesses, (6) disclosure of all adverse evidence, (7) the right to an attorney if desired, (8) a decision based solely on the evidence produced at the hearing, (9) a statement of the reasons for the decision, and (10)—of course—an impartial decision maker. Elaborating on the impartiality required, the Court observed that although "prior involvement in some aspects of a case will not necessarily bar a welfare official from acting as a decision maker," the official must not "have participated in making the determination under review"; that is, the judge must not be reviewing his own decision.[6]

Not only did the Court in *Goldberg* define the procedure

---

difficulties of distinguishing procedure from substance, the case seemed to some observers, even to some of the justices, to involve substantive due process (at 599 [Scalia, J., dissenting] and at 612 [Ginsburg, J., dissenting]). See also Phillips, *The* Lochner *Court*, 41–44.

[5]397 U.S. 254 (1970).

[6]Ibid., at 271.

due process requires, but it also recognized a new substance: "Welfare benefits," the Court concluded, "are a matter of statutory entitlement for persons qualified to receive them."[7] Taking away such benefits could be accomplished only by means modeled on taking away property. Although a legal maxim since the days of Coke had proclaimed "ubi jus, ibi remedium" (where there is a right, there is a remedy),[8] the converse is also true: "Where there is a remedy, there is a right."[9] With typical bluntness, Oliver Wendell Holmes once described a legal right as "only the hypostasis of a prophecy—the imagination of a substance supporting the fact that the public force will be brought to bear upon those who do things said to contravene it."[10] Given comparable protection, welfare benefits became in effect a new form of property; thus did procedure turn into substance.[11] Benefits as property and not as mere gratuity remains one of the pillars of the modern wel-

[7]Ibid., at 262.

[8]Edward Coke, *Commentary upon Littleton* (London, 1628), 197a. See also Herbert Broom, *Legal Maxims,* 8th American ed. (Philadelphia, 1882), 191.

[9]See Frederick Pollock and Frederic Maitland, *The History of English Law,* 2d ed. (Cambridge, 1898), 2: 31. See also John V. Orth, *The Judicial Power of the United States: The Eleventh Amendment in American History* (New York: Oxford University Press, 1987), 4–5, 52, 107.

[10]O. W. Holmes, "Natural Law," *Harvard Law Review* 32 (1918): 42.

[11]See Charles Reich, "The New Property," *Yale Law Journal* 73 (1964): 733–87, and "Individual Rights and Social Welfare: The Emerging Legal Issues," *Yale Law Journal* 74 (1965): 1245–57. Reich's articles were cited by the Court in *Goldberg,* 397 U.S., at 262 n. 8. Reich's property law theories

fare state, still standing although eroded by later restrictive rulings.[12]

Case II: Taking from A and Giving to B

Taking from A and giving to B did not disappear as a problem simply because the U.S. Supreme Court stopped talking about it in 1938, but the *Carolene Products* case did mean that the Court would no longer look for violations in ordinary regulatory legislation as it had during the *Lochner* era.[13] The paradigm itself still sometimes appears in the reports, usually in quotations from earlier cases. In 1998, for example, the Supreme Court invalidated part of a federal statute dealing with retirees' benefits in the coal industry, quoting in passing from Justice Samuel Chase's discourse in *Calder v. Bull:* "'It is against all reason and justice' to presume that the legislature has been entrusted with the power to enact 'a

---

are criticized by Philip K. Howard, *The Death of Common Sense: How Law Is Suffocating America* (New York: Random House, 1995). Reich's more general social theories, expressed in his best-selling book, *The Greening of America* (New York: Random House, 1970), are attacked by Roger Kimball, *The Long March* (San Francisco: Encounter Books, 2000).

[12]E.g., *Mathews v. Eldridge,* 424 U.S. 319 (1976) (permitting termination of disability benefits before an evidentiary hearing).

[13]One commentator has observed a "slow return of economic substantive due process." See Phillips, *The* Lochner *Court,* 41–44, 192–96.

law that takes property from A and gives it to B.'"[14] A few years earlier, the North Carolina Supreme Court had invalidated part of a state statute dealing with the ownership of land under a railroad right-of-way by quoting from a hundred-year-old case that had quoted in turn from Justice Story's decision in *Wilkinson v. Leland:* "We know of no case, in which a legislative act to transfer the property of A to B without his consent, has ever been held a constitutional exercise of legislative power in any state in the Union."[15] Wrenched from its original context, Story's dictum is now understood as referring to legislative confiscation rather than merely to legislative interference in the judicial process.

In 1967 Hawaii passed a land reform act designed to break up large estates, a remnant of that state's semifeudal past, by giving lessees of single family homes the right to purchase the property they leased, even if the landowner refused to sell. A federal court of appeals found the act unconstitutional, "a naked attempt on the part of the state of Hawaii to take the private property of A and transfer it to B solely for B's private use and benefit."[16] The A-to-B paradigm was invoked here not in a substantive due process

[14]*Eastern Enterprises v. Apfel,* 524 U.S. 498, 523 (1998).

[15]*McDonald's Corp. v. Dwyer,* 450 S.E.2d 888, 891 (N.C. 1994) (quoting *Trustees of the University of North Carolina v. North Carolina R.R. Co.,* 76 N.C. 103, 107 [1877]). The quotation was modified in insignificant ways in transmission.

[16]*Midkiff v. Tom,* 702 F.2d 788, 798 (9th Cir. 1983).

case properly so called, but in a case arising under the Fifth Amendment's takings clause, applied to the states by the Fourteenth Amendment. The problem with the statute, in the appellate court's view, was not so much that property was taken—just compensation was, after all, required—but that the use to be made of the property was "private" rather than "public." Reversing the court of appeals and upholding the Hawaii statute, the U.S. Supreme Court dispensed with the A-to-B paradigm and held that a use is sufficiently public whenever it is rationally related to some conceivable public purpose. Henceforth, the Court said, the judiciary should defer to the legislature on the question, unless the state's claim is without any reasonable foundation—a standard analogous to that announced thirty years earlier in *Carolene Products* with respect to regulatory legislation and the due process clause.[17]

Now that substantive due process is almost exclusively concerned with noneconomic rights, the takings clause has gained new salience in economic cases. Regulatory legislation, once challenged as a violation of due process and invoking the generic A-to-B paradigm, is now challenged under the takings clause, spawning the concept of a "regulatory taking," that is, a government regulation that restricts the use of property, usually land, so as to diminish its market value without compensation. Much of the debate has centered on the question whether the regulation operates to im-

[17] *Hawaii Housing Authority v. Midkiff,* 467 U.S. 229 (1984).

pose on a small group burdens that should be borne by the public at large. In this guise, taking from A and giving to B, once the touchstone in substantive due process cases, has reappeared in cases arising under the takings clause.[18] Likewise, zoning, which had once raised questions of due process, is now challenged as an uncompensated taking.[19] Because state courts sometimes reject claims of regulatory takings by holding that the property right in question never existed or was previously extinguished, the suggestion has been made, even in the highest judicial circles, that there may be such a thing as a judicial as well as a legislative taking.[20]

---

[18]Compare *Seawall Assocs. v. City of New York*, 542 N.E.2d 1059, 1069 (1989) (holding city ordinance prohibiting landlords from ceasing to rent single rooms a violation of the takings clause because "the obligations placed on a few property owners are just the kind which could, and should, be borne by the taxpayers as a whole") with *Adkins v. Children's Hospital*, 261 U.S. 525, 557–58 (1923) (holding statute setting minimum wage for women a violation of the due process clause because it amounts to "a compulsory exaction from the employer for the support of a partially indigent person, for whose condition there rests upon him no peculiar responsibility, and therefore, in effect, arbitrarily shifts to his shoulders a burden which, if it belongs to anybody, belongs to society as a whole").

[19]Compare *Village of Euclid v. Ambler Realty Co.*, 272 U.S. 365 (1926) (rejecting challenges based on the due process clause, the equal protection clause, and the takings clause) with *Lucas v. South Carolina Coastal Council*, 505 U.S. 1003 (1992) (finding possible violation of the takings clause) and *Palazzolo v. Rhode Island*, 533 U.S. 592 (2001) (same).

[20]*Stevens v. Cannon Beach*, 510 U.S. 1207 (1994) (Scalia, J., dissenting from the denial of a petition for a writ of certiorari). The title to the same real estate was also involved in *State ex rel. Thornton v. Hay*, 462 P.2d 671 (Or. 1969), cited in chapter 2, as an example of a case in which a modern court used custom as a source of law.

Although the due process clause does not actually contain the word, "taking" has long been part of its vocabulary by association with the case once commonly used to illustrate its violation, an association even more inescapable since the Fourteenth Amendment, unlike the Fifth Amendment, does not include a takings clause as such. In state constitutions that lack an express takings clause, the guarantee of due process (or the law of the land) must do double duty.[21] Likewise, in federal court, state takings without compensation or for purposes that are not public must be tested under the due process clause of the Fourteenth Amendment, at one time because such takings would violate the due process clause itself (as in the state constitutions just mentioned),[22] today because the due process clause of

---

[21]See, e.g., *Johnston v. Rankin,* 70 N.C. 550 (1874) ("notwithstanding there is no clause in the Constitution of North Carolina which expressly prohibits private property from being taken without compensation . . . , yet the principle is so grounded in natural equity that it had never been denied to be part of the law of North Carolina"), and *Finch v. Durham,* 384 S.E.2d 8 (N.C. 1989) (same). See John V. Orth, *The North Carolina State Constitution: A Reference Guide* (Westport, Conn.: Greenwood Press, 1993), 58. Although it once had company, North Carolina is today the last state without an express takings clause in its constitution. See Philip Nichols, *The Law of Eminent Domain,* ed. Julius L. Sackman and Russell D. Van Brunt, 3d ed. (Albany, N.Y., 2000), vol. 1, § 4.8.

[22]See *Pennsylvania Coal Co. v. Mahon,* 260 U.S. 393 (1922). Although now viewed as an early example of a "regulatory takings" case, *Mahon* was treated by its author, Justice Oliver Wendell Holmes, as a due process case. See also *Chicago, Burlington & Quincy R.R. v. Chicago,* 166 U.S. 226 (1897). Although now viewed as an early example of "incorporation," that is, reading the restraints on the federal government contained in the Bill

the Fourteenth Amendment incorporates and applies to the states the takings clause of the Fifth Amendment.[23]

Takings, once treated generically for due process purposes, are now best considered under two species. The state takes property under the takings clause if it is useful to the public, and pays just compensation; it takes things under the due process clause if they are harmful, and pays nothing at all.[24] Takings under the due process clause, in the exercise of the state's police power, may involve the taking of tangible property, as for example contraband, in which case actual possession is transferred to the state; or they may involve taking—in the sense of "taking away"—claimed rights, in which case there is no transfer: there may be a loss (a taking) but there is no corresponding gain (a giving).[25]

---

of Rights into the Fourteenth Amendment and thereby making them applicable to the states, the *Chicago Railroad* case was in its day also viewed as a straightforward due process case.

[23]When the role of the due process clause of the Fourteenth Amendment is to apply to the states' parts of the Bill of Rights, as in *Griswold v. Connecticut* (the birth control case), due process is not "substantive"; that is, it does not serve as an independent source of restrictions but as a mere conduit for other, substantial rights.

[24]Ernst Freund, *The Police Power, Public Policy and Constitutional Rights* (Chicago: Callaghan, 1904), § 511 ("the state takes property by eminent domain because it is useful to the public, and under the police power because it is harmful"). The takings clause of the Fifth Amendment refers specifically (and exclusively) to property, and the due process clause refers comprehensively to life, liberty, or property.

[25]In technical terms, if a right is recognized—as the freedom to contract concerning hours of labor was recognized in *Lochner*—then the state

Case III: Taking from A

Taking from A never quite made the anthology of legal maxims. By the time of its emergence, maxims had gone out of fashion, but its essence remains and continues to trouble the public pulse, particularly in cases concerning personal rights implicating important moral values. Although *Griswold v. Connecticut*, the birth control case, was ostensibly decided on other grounds, it is now recognized as a substantive due process decision, and the famous (or infamous) abortion case, *Roe v. Wade*, was frankly rested on the due process clause. By narrow majorities, the U.S. Supreme Court has rejected due process challenges to laws prohibiting professional medical assistance in the commission of suicide ("the right to die")[26] and laws outlawing homosexual acts even between consenting adults in private ("gay rights").[27] In such cases there was, at least in contemplation of law, no taking because there was no right in the first place. Further attempts to invoke the due process clause by unpopular minorities, erotic or otherwise, and by advocates of other practices challenging majority values can confidently be predicted.

---

may take it away only by "due process of law." By contrast, if no right is recognized—as none was in the *Carolene Products* case—then there was nothing to be taken by the legislation.

[26] *Washington v. Glucksberg,* 521 U.S. 702 (1997).

[27] *Bowers v. Hardwick,* 478 U.S. 186 (1986).

In a curious way, the taking-from-A paradigm has returned due process to its roots. The Fifth Amendment, added to the U.S. Constitution as part of the Bill of Rights in 1791 and applicable only to the federal government, provides that "no person shall . . . be deprived of life, liberty, or property, without due process of law," and the Fourteenth Amendment, adopted in 1868, extends the same prohibition to the states. The A-to-B paradigm, despite its centuries-long association with due process, added an element missing from the original formulation: the element of transfer, an element that might never have surfaced if the paradigm had not gained currency. Transfer is of the essence of contract, traditionally defined as a "bargained for exchange," and it is hardly accidental that the A-to-B paradigm flourished during the ascendancy of contract in American law and helped usher in the era of freedom of contract. The demise of economic substantive due process meant a renewed interest in what is taken by government action, regardless of whether it is given to another or not and regardless of whether it has obvious economic value or not. Ironically, the historic zeal to protect private property aided in the transformation of the due process clause, once the watchdog of the free market, into the guardian of privacy in intimate personal relations. Taking away rights, whether by the legislature or by the executive, must be justified and may not be arbitrary, although without the economic context a generally accepted standard for arbitrariness has been hard to find.

Words have meanings, so the phrase "due process of law" must have content, or (if you will) substance. In the long history of due process, the procedural content certainly came first: the requirement to proceed only "by the law of the land," wrung from a reluctant King John in Magna Carta, limited the way the sovereign could deal with his subjects. Although procedure may seem to be an obvious matter of form rather than substance, in public affairs it may implicate ends as well as means. That the English king could not make a man a judge in his own case meant among other things that he could not influence the outcome of a case simply by choosing the judge who would decide it or in a case involving himself and his subjects simply decide it himself. That an American state must provide a fair hearing before terminating welfare benefits signaled the recognition of a legal right to such benefits. But due process in America has substance beyond the derivative substance just mentioned. Just as Magna Carta's Latin phrase "per legem terrae" (by the law of the land) yielded to Sir Edward Coke's English translation "due process of law," so the paradigm of what due process prohibited enlarged to include not only the procedural horror of making a man a judge in his own case but also the ambiguous one of taking from A and giving to B. And just as the primitive royal government of early medieval England yielded to lawmaking by representative assemblies, so the strictures of due process bound legislatures as well as kings and their modern executive counter-parts. As Justice Miller observed in *Davidson v. New Orleans* more than a century ago, American states cannot do any-thing they please just because they follow proper procedures.

The common law, the "law of the land," was anterior to all constitutions. In England, still lacking a written consti-tution, the common law itself supplied the rules now de-scribed as constitutional. As one influential English scholar put it, "The general principles of the constitution" are— "like all maxims established by judicial legislation"—mere generalizations from "judicial decisions determining the rights of private persons in particular cases."[28] As late as the time of Coke, the relationship between common law and statute law was still unclear. In America the U.S. Constitu-tion declared itself "the supreme law of the land,"[29] and con-stitutional amendments added the guarantee of due process. That meant, in turn, that the judges would test legislation against the norms of the common law.[30] The ragged dis-putes that followed about the meaning of due process wit-ness to the uneven join of common law and constitution.

Though Sir Edward Coke was concerned about the abuse of political power (making a man a judge in his own

[28]A. V. Dicey, *Introduction to the Study of the Law of the Constitution*, 7th ed. (London: Macmillan, 1908), 191–92.

[29]U.S. Constitution, Art. 6.

[30]See, e.g., *State v. Anonymous*, 2 N.C. 28, 29 (1794) (the law of the land means "according to the course of the common law"). North Carolina's influential chief justice Thomas Ruffin stated the matter forcefully in an

case) and nineteenth-century jurists about sound economics (taking from A and giving to B), post-1937 judges have been concerned about invasions of individual rights (taking from A). Somehow the underlying concerns—perhaps what successive judges thought Justice Chase had in mind when referring to "the first great principles of the social compact"—have a way of finding expression in constitutional terms. "Due process of law" long summed them all up, but other clauses have lately been pressed into service as well. What was once considered a due process problem may today be addressed as a takings problem or an equal protection problem (and vice versa).

Taking from A and giving to B has illustrated an abuse of power ever since the founding of the Republic. Although without an express reference in the constitutional texts, it soon found a home in the due process (law of the land) clauses. To that extent substantive due process was coeval in this country with its procedural counterpart, making a man a judge in his own case, which also lacked an express reference. But the A-to-B paradigm proved ambiguous in a way

---

important case: "Such legislative acts, as profess in themselves directly to punish persons or to deprive the citizen of his property, without trial before the judicial tribunals, and a decision upon the matter of right, as determined by the laws under which it vested, according to the course, mode and usages of the common law as derived from our forefathers, are not effectually 'laws of the land' for those purposes" (*Hoke v. Henderson*, 15 N.C. 1, 16 [1834]). See Orth, *The North Carolina State Constitution*, 55–59.

that the judge in his own case never was. Over time, the emphasis in the taking paradigm shifted from denying legislative determination of title, essentially a judicial function, to denying legislative interference with economic enterprise. Once the shift was complete, substantive due process had emerged to parallel procedural due process. Within substantive due process, in turn, the transactional emphasis implicit in the A-to-B paradigm led to an emphasis on freedom of contract that eventually caused a further shift to the simpler taking-from-A paradigm, and the emphasis on intention implicit in contract law facilitated legal recognition of the expectation of individual privacy. When substantive due process was eventually abandoned as a check on ordinary regulatory legislation, the category was not closed altogether; instead, substantive due process was divided into economic substantive due process—now largely inactive—and noneconomic (or social) substantive due process, a continuing and contentious source of constitutional development.

It is difficult to imagine the emergence of further paradigms to guide the future development of due process; on the one hand, mature legal systems generate more elaborate statements of fundamental principles than simple maxims, and on the other, the taking-from-A paradigm is already expressed at such a high level of abstraction that it offers little practical direction. Due process forbids arbitrary government action that takes (or significantly impairs) life, liberty, or property—or their functional equivalents or necessary adjuncts. The social values involved must be of great importance, essential to personal autonomy, what freedom of contract was during the *Lochner* era and what the right of privacy is today.

The details of future developments cannot be specified, but the means by which they will be elucidated are obvious. When due process of law was adopted as a constitutional standard in America, it came accompanied by the common law method of case-by-case decision making. "Like cases should be decided alike," but since no two cases are exactly alike, common law precedents form a linked chain of reasoning. Although the first links may not closely resemble the last, first and last are connected in a continuous series. There is nothing inevitable about this concatenation; mistakes have been (and will be) made. But the standard of due process is not formulated anew at each judicial generation; it is connected, for better or worse, to what went before. Just as taking from A and giving to B was recognized as a violation of due process because it was just as bad as making a man a judge in his own case, and just as taking from A and giving to B yielded to taking from A, so new claims of due process violations will be judged by comparison with old. Whether encapsulated in simple paradigms or found in more convoluted statements, the past will necessarily shape the future demands of due process.

Selected Bibliography

Bewig, Matthew S. "Lochner v. The Journeymen Bakers of New York: The Journeymen Bakers, Their Hours of Labor, and the Constitution," *American Journal of Legal History* 38 (1994): 413–51.

Cook, Harold J. "Against Common Right and Reason: The Royal College of Physicians Versus Doctor Thomas Bonham," *American Journal of Legal History* 29 (1985): 301–22.

Corwin, Edward S. "The 'Higher Law' Background of American Constitutional Law," *Harvard Law Review* 42 (1928–1929): 149–85, 365–409.

———. *Liberty Against Government.* Baton Rouge: Louisiana State University Press, 1948.

Ely, James W. "Economic Due Process Revisited," *Vanderbilt Law Review* 44 (1991): 213–20.

———. "The Oxymoron Reconsidered: Myth and Reality in

the Origins of Substantive Due Process," *Constitutional Commentary* 16 (1999): 315–45.

Gilman, Howard. *The Constitution Besieged: The Rise and Demise of Lochner Era Police Powers Jurisprudence.* Durham, N.C.: Duke University Press, 1993.

Gough, J. W. *Fundamental Law in English Constitutional History.* Oxford: Clarendon Press, 1955.

Gray, Charles M. "Bonham's Case Reviewed," *Proceedings of the American Philosophical Society* 116 (1972): 35–58.

Harrison, John. "Substantive Due Process and the Constitutional Text," *Virginia Law Review* 83 (1997): 493–558.

Hovenkamp, Herbert. "The Political Economy of Substantive Due Process," *Stanford Law Review* 40 (1988): 379–447.

Kens, Paul. *Judicial Power and Reform Politics: The Anatomy of Lochner v. New York.* Lawrence: University Press of Kansas, 1990.

McCormack, Wayne. "Economic Substantive Due Process and the Right of Livelihood," *Kentucky Law Journal* 82 (1993): 397–463.

Mendelson, Wallace. "A Missing Link in the Evolution of Due Process," *Vanderbilt Law Review* 10 (1956): 125–37.

Orth, John V. "Contract and the Common Law," in *The State and Freedom of Contract*, ed. Harry N. Scheiber. Stanford: Stanford University Press, 1998, 44–65.

———. "Did Sir Edward Coke Mean What He Said?" *Constitutional Commentary* 16 (1999): 33–38.

———. "Exporting the Rule of Law," *North Carolina Journal of International Law* 24 (1998): 71–82.

———. "Taking from A and Giving to B: Substantive Due Process and the Case of the Shifting Paradigm," *Constitutional Commentary* 14 (1997): 337–45.

———. *The North Carolina State Constitution: A Reference Guide.* Westport, Conn.: Greenwood Press, 1993.

Phillips, Michael J. *The* Lochner *Court, Myth and Reality: Substantive Due Process from the 1890s to the 1930s.* Westport, Conn.: Praeger, 2001.

Post, Robert C. "Defending the Lifeworld: Substantive Due Process in the Taft Court Era," *Boston College Law Review* 78 (1998): 1489–545.

Pound, Roscoe. "Liberty of Contract," *Yale Law Journal* 18 (1909): 454–87.

Riggs, Robert E. "Substantive Due Process in 1791," *Wisconsin Law Review* (1990): 941–1004.

Siegel, Stephen A. "*Lochner* Era Jurisprudence and the American Constitutional Tradition," *North Carolina Law Review* 70 (1991): 1–111.

Stoner, James, Jr. *Common Law and Liberal Theory: Coke, Hobbes, and the Origins of American Constitutionalism.* Lawrence: University Press of Kansas, 1992.

Strong, Frank R. *Substantive Due Process of Law: A Dichotomy of Sense and Nonsense.* Durham, N.C.: Carolina Academic Press, 1986.

Thorne, Samuel. "Dr. Bonham's Case," *Law Quarterly Review* 54 (1938): 543–52.

Yale, D. E. C. "*Iudex in Propria Causa:* An Historical Excursus," *Cambridge Law Journal* 33 (1974): 80–96.

Table of Cases

Index